Wildfight

A History of Conservation

Wildfight

A History of Conservation

COLIN WILLOCK

JONATHAN CAPE
LONDON

First published 1991
© Colin Willock 1991
Jonathan Cape, 20 Vauxhall Bridge Road, London SW1V 2SA

Colin Willock has asserted his right
under the Copyright, Designs and Patents Act, 1988
to be identified as the author of this work

A CIP catalogue record for this book
is available from the British Library

ISBN 0–224–02774–3

Phototypeset by Computape (Pickering) Ltd, North Yorkshire
Printed in Great Britain by
Butler & Tanner Ltd, Frome and London

Contents

For our Grandchildren
Mark
David
James
Emma
William
who have a love of the natural
world and must learn to guard it well

Acknowledgments

First and foremost I must thank Survival Anglia, makers of the longest running British television wildlife series, for sending me – and frequently my wife – to some of the wildest places left on earth where we filmed many of the events and people described in this book. I particularly wish to thank the several experts, scientists as well as national park wardens, who put up with my persistent questioning. I owe a great deal to the wildlife cameramen with whom I shared safaris and adventures, most of all to Dieter Plage, Des Bartlett, Alan Root and Friedemann Koester. In the company of these and others I learned about conservation from the sharp end. Despite these experiences in the field I found, when I came to write this book, that there were large gaps in my knowledge. These were willingly filled in by many experts, colleagues and friends. Ian MacPhail, former International Campaigns Director of the World Wildlife Fund, recalled for me the heady early days of that organisation; Michael Ounsted, Developments Officer of the Wildfowl and Wetlands Trust, explained the intricacies and pitfalls involved in reintroducing endangered species to the wild; Ian Player, former head warden of the Natal Parks and founder of the Wilderness Leadership School in Natal, gave me much help about the early days of hunting and conservation in South Africa; Lyn de Alwis, retired head of the Sri Lankan National Parks, gave me up-to-date information on the elephant rescue and movement operation which we filmed at Deduru-Oya; and David Hopcraft, who farms game animals on the Athi Plains in Kenya, gave me permission to quote from his researches. I also gratefully acknowledge the kindness of the editor of *Oryx*, journal of the Fauna and Flora Preservation Society, who allowed me to quote freely from his pages; and Harvey Nelson, co-editor of *Flyways* published by the US Fish and Wildlife Service.

Picture Credits

The author and publishers are grateful for permission to reproduce the following illustrations: Africana Museum (4); Associated Press (5, 6); Anthony Bannister, NHPA (20); Jen & Des Bartlett, Survival Anglia (3, 14); Joe Blossom, Wildfowl & Wetlands Trust (17); Bob Campbell, Survival Anglia (13); J. Allan Cash, Survival Anglia (7); Mary Evans Picture Library (2); Jeff Foott, Survival Anglia (1); Grzimek, Okapia Frankfurt (10, 11, 12); Dieter Plage, Survival Anglia (22, 23, 28); Dieter & Mary Plage, Survival Anglia (18); Popperfoto (24, 26, 27); Jonathan Scott, Planet Earth Pictures (21); Philippa Scott (25); Survival Anglia (8); Syndication International (9); Weyler, Greenpeace (29); Colin Willock (15, 19).

Introduction

In the 27 years I spent writing and producing wildlife documentaries for the television series 'Survival', I was lucky enough to travel to some of the world's wildest places and make the close, sometimes too close, acquaintance of some of its wildest and rarest animals on earth. Those exciting years coincided with the growth and spread of the world conservation movement.

In my more cynical moments I sometimes wondered whether it was all worthwhile and whether the tremendous efforts being made to save the world's wildlife weren't just a sentimental exercise. The argument I had with myself in those moments of depression went like this.

Homo sapiens has emerged as the dominant species on Planet Earth. The role of a dominant species is to dominate, at least until it becomes effete and is replaced by a more successful one. Though there may now be signs of effetism in the human race, there is, as yet, no sign of a replacement. This being true, those species that can't compete with *Homo sapiens* don't deserve to survive. If they had been smart enough to invent the nuclear power station or even the chainsaw, then they might have had a fighting chance. But they weren't and so they can't expect evolutionary processes to show them any mercy. In nature, those who don't adapt go to the wall. If they can't save themselves, then why should the dominant species bother about doing it for them?

It is an argument of sorts but it leaves out one very important factor. The instrument that enables man to dominate is his brain. Never mind how this amazing computer evolved. Perhaps cerebral development began when our ancestors first stood upright, thus freeing their hands to manipulate tools, starting with the stone axe. I suppose we will never precisely know. Leave that to the palaeontologists to argue about. What is certain is that somewhere in that magic box of tricks called the cerebrum is a department labelled 'awareness' and maybe even 'conscience'. This is as much a part of the dominant species' mental make-up as is the technical brilliance that enables it to build Concorde. We have only very recently, within the last hundred years at the very outside, discovered this compartment in the brain and begun to apply it to conservation. It is this conscience that now encourages us to conserve rather than to destroy wildlife.

Why are we concerned at all? There seems little doubt that the majority of people in the Western world like the idea of wildlife surviving to share the planet with them. They have a basic sympathy with animals that is by no means shared in poorer, less developed countries. This regard for animals may only manifest itself in keeping a pet. Nevertheless it is a short step from enjoying the company of a dog, cat or even a budgie to feeling a pang of regret if their pets' wild relatives are in danger of disappearing from the face of the earth. For the cause of conservation it is fortunate that these feelings exist mainly in Western nations who are better able to afford and support 'saving' operations.

There are deeper reasons why so many people feel an empathy with wild animals struggling to exist in an ever-contracting world. Between wildlife and ourselves is a subconscious connection that stretches back to our own origins. However dimly, most of us occasionally glimpse the shadowy figure back there in the trees, or even up in the trees, that was our distant forbear. We sense that wildlife and humans are all part of the same living scene and that we should therefore strive to see that the other actors have at least a walk-on part. In a more cynical though practical vein, we could view wildlife as a kind of litmus paper with which we test our own chances of survival on earth. Instead of turning red or blue like the litmus, wildlife just disappears. When it has all gone ask yourself this question: 'Who's next?'

At first, for most people, conservation simply meant saving wild animals. Their plight could be readily understood and saving them was the focus point for both moral and material public support. Now it is recognised that conservation must also be applied to the environment in which both wildlife and we ourselves live. There is little doubt that this enlargement of public awareness would never have come about had not the original emphasis been on protecting the panda, the rhino, the whale, the elephant and many more species beleagured in the wild. It is scarcely an exaggeration to say that the Green Movement itself owes its origins to public concern for vanishing wildlife. The realisation that it is as important to protect the environment, including the atmosphere and the oceans, as it is to conserve our flora and fauna now affects our entire life style. It influences what we eat and drink, what we buy and wear, and for whom we vote.

Having said all that, and having acknowledged the scope and power of the Green Movement, let us return to the bedrock of conservation, protecting wildlife. This book tells the story of the most important 'saving' operations in recent conservation history and of the techniques used. Inevitably it deals with failures, the mistakes made and lessons learned. It also deals with triumphs, if only on a limited front.

As these stories unfold, the problems facing the conservationists emerge. One or, more often, a combination of such problems occurs in every case. Common to each operation aimed at saving wildlife is the fact that man's interests, often in making a fast buck for himself, have clashed with and taken precedence over the needs of wild animals and places. All too often this means that he either slaughters the animals or destroys the habitat in which they live.

Sometimes, the clash of interests is justifiable from a human standpoint. Under-privileged people often have to get a precarious living from land that is occupied by wildlife. If those people's welfare, let alone their survival, is at stake, then these must take priority. Occasionally a compromise can be found but, in a world in which over-population is a major cause of starvation and land hunger, this is increasingly hard to bring about.

Conservation itself has many problems yet to solve. Scientists will readily admit that still too little is known about the ecology of some threatened species. Scientific knowledge often lags behind the operation that is being mounted to save an endangered animal. Perhaps the largest overall problem is one of education, not only of the general public, but also of industry and governments. These latter have it in their power to do the most damage as well as the most good.

The people involved in conservation are as important as the techniques they use. I have had the good fortune to work in the field with a good many of the key figures. The book describes what they did not only to save and protect animals but to influence people and organisations to take a favourable view of conserving wildlife and wild places.

Unfortunately, while the aims of conservation are great, its financial means remain depressingly small. Achievement is, therefore, always going to be limited. While some of the events related in this book were truly spectacular and gratifyingly successful, seen in the perspective of the whole they can only be regarded as patches on an ark that is leaking badly in many places. The ark is, however, still afloat and it is vital not to become discouraged and to give up the repair work. Despite the number of new leaks that have been sprung in the conservation ark's hull, it is without doubt floating higher in the water than it was 30 years ago.

I

The Years of Overkill

It is always difficult to pinpoint the beginnings of a movement and the conservation movement is no exception. The concept of saving wild animals from destruction, or even extinction, is not very old. It is not hard to see why. Until a little over a century ago there seemed to be no reason to make the effort. There was more than enough wildlife, everywhere, to go round. Man could still hunt and kill indiscriminately without apparently doing any permanent damage.

So what in the last hundred years has changed, some would say at far too slow a pace, in our pattern of thinking? There were many contributory factors, but there has to be a central one. I believe that this was, beyond any doubt, a reaction to what I think of as the years of the Great Slaughter. This was the period between 1800 and the early 1900s when man wiped out animals on a colossal scale. Though the word had not yet been used in a wildlife context, conservation came about as a direct reaction to that slaughter. It certainly didn't happen as if man's attitude to the natural world had altered in a blinding flash of light. The conservation movement gathered force gradually and largely through the efforts of a handful of far-sighted men who could see what their native wilderness would become if the slaughter was not halted and the ravages repaired wherever possible.

Although nowadays we do our share of wiping out species, this is usually through pollution or destruction of habitat. The years of the Great Slaughter were different and in some ways easier to understand. The motivation was greed backed by total lack of recognition of the consequences. The instrument of destruction was the gun and the outcome something which Adolf Hitler might have envied – a final solution for a whole race or species.

Before you can begin to consider what we are doing now in an attempt to save the world's remaining wildlife, it is important to appreciate the enormity of the crimes we have committed against animals in the recent past. The Great Slaughter took place on land, in the sea, and among the birds of the air. On land, it happened at a rate which even the killers found baffling. In terms of wildlife genocide nothing, not even the current slaughter of the African elephant for ivory, can compare with the near extinction of the American bison, popularly called the buffalo. In the sheer volume of animals slain nothing like it had been seen before and, with any luck, will never be seen again. Experts still argue about how many there were. Estimates vary between 60 million, probably an overstatement, to 20 million, almost certainly an underestimate. Even 20 million is a lot of buffalo. Nevertheless, it is only a statistic. It cannot begin to convey what those millions looked like even when spread over the vast expanses of the central plains and reaching from Texas in the south to Canada in the north. Early travellers tried to describe them: 'As numerous as the locusts of Egypt', 'We could not see their limit either north or west', 'The plains were black and appeared to be in motion'. Perhaps most graphic of all: 'The country was one great buffalo robe'.

Many of these early accounts were dismissed back east as wild travellers' tales. When the easterners themselves moved west in the course of opening up the new country, they discovered that these descriptions were a mere synopsis of the true story. River steamers were sometimes stopped dead in midstream by dense masses of swimming buffalo. When 50,000 buffalo decided to cross the rail tracks, a train could be held up for hours or even days. Neither train nor steamboat was to be delayed for long. The same technology that had produced these new means of rapid travel was busy turning out the .44 Remington and Springfield rifles and the most famous buffalo gun of all, The Big Fifty, properly known as the Sharps .50–100 after the calibre of its bullet and the weight of powder in its load. In a few short years these rifles would clear the tracks and waterways of obstruction by buffalo.

The same pioneering spirit that drove the railroads westwards inspired the settlers and adventurers who travelled on them. These men came with their families first by Conestoga wagon and later by train to set up as farmers and ranchers. Buffalo, farming and ranching were inevitably on a collision course. All the same, the Great Slaughter did not begin with any such reasonably understandable motives but because buffalo hunting was a quick way to earn a buck.

First in the game were the mountain men, the beaver hunters. When the bottom dropped out of the beaver market around 1840, these wild men turned from trapping beaver for their pelts to hunting buffalo for their hides. Some of the settlers who had come to farm found the land too poor or hard to work and turned to buffalo shooting. After all, they had to survive somehow. In 1840, 400 mounted hunters of the Red River Hunting Expedition brought back over one million pounds of buffalo meat from the plains of Manitoba and the Dakota Territory which they sold to the Hudson's Bay Company.

Then came the noblemen from Europe to hunt for sport, men like St George Gore from Ireland who set out in 1854 from St Louis with a retinue of 40 servants. One entire wagon was needed to carry his muzzle-loading guns, 75 rifles in all. By the time Gore disbanded his expedition three years later he had killed 2,000 buffalo. Others followed. William Drummond from Scotland hunted in a white jacket and Panama hat and boasted that he had left the prairie around the River Platte 'strewn for miles with buffalo carcases'. The exploits of these men inspired the railroad companies to sell low-cost hunting-by-train excursions across the Kansas prairies. The 'sportsmen' fired from the carriage windows, leaving the bodies to rot by the side of the track. Seldom did the train stop to take a dead buffalo aboard.

The Civil War put an end to the fun. The real kill came in the 1870s when the professional hunters moved in on a seemingly endless resource. It is highly probable that these men had no conception that they were literally wiping out their source of income. Many were under the impression that they were simply harvesting the buffalos' annual increase. On the Great Plains, the height of the slaughter came between 1872 and 1874. At least 4 million buffalo were killed during that period. Often, only the tongue was removed for pickling and the rest of the meat left to rot. The tanneries of Europe had perfected a new process for turning buffalo hides into fine leather. The thickly-furred winter hides were made into luxury robes. Business for the hunter boomed; so did his gun. The hunters seldom became rich. Their trade was, however, one of the few thriving ones in the depression that hit the States in 1873.

The Great Plains were shot out by 1877 so the hunters moved into the southern range and slaughtered the Texas herds. The crack shots, men like Tom Nixon and Orlando 'Brick' Bond, killed 200 buffalo at a single stand. The art was to shoot the animals, cleanly, one by one where they stood so that they fell dead without stampeding the rest of the herd. The real professionals only killed as many animals in a day as their skinners could deal with but it was enough to put paid to the southern range and after that to the northern herds as well. The railroads had already divided the buffalo into northern and southern concentrations. Once the hunters decided to clean up the

3

northern herd they killed 70,000 animals in a single season.

Towards the end, political motives speeded the slaughter. The Plains Indians, tribes like the Sioux, the Cheyenne, the Arapaho and the Kiowa were the perfect example of peoples in balance with their ecology. We could learn from them today. Tom McHugh, biologist, film-maker and expert on the buffalo, has described their relationship with the Great Plains perfectly in his book *The Time of the Buffalo*.

> The tribes became as much part of the plains community as the grasses, pronghorn antelope, the prairie dogs and the buffalo themselves, for they learned how to belong to the land as well as take from it. The buffalo with whom they shared their domain became linked with them in a unique physical and spiritual relationship. Buffalo were the Indians' commissary, furnishing, food, clothing, shelter and a remarkable range of luxury articles, but there was more to the relationship between the Indian and the beast than such material considerations. The daily thought and ceremonial practices of the tribe, indeed their very culture, developed out of their response to the buffalo.

It didn't take the military mind long to work out that the surest way to defeat the plains Indian was to wipe out his supply of food and clothing. In 1874 General Phil Sheridan blocked a Congressional bill aimed at saving the last of the dwindling herds with these words: 'Instead of stopping the hunters they ought to give them a hearty unanimous vote of thanks ... For the sake of lasting peace, let them kill, skin and sell until the buffalo are exterminated. Then your prairies can be covered with speckled cattle and the festive cowboy.'

When the last buffalo had been shot the hunters were replaced by the scavengers. First came the 'wolvers' who poisoned rotting buffalo carcases in the hope that wolves would eat the carrion and die. Wolf skins fetched a dollar a piece. The poison killed many creatures besides wolves – coyotes, badgers, ravens and birds of prey.

These ghouls were followed by the bone-pickers. Buffalo bones fetched between $8 and $20 a ton. At one railhead there stood a pile of bones 60 feet high and half a mile long. Some scavengers even pulled off the hair still clinging to buffalo skulls and sold it at 75 cents a pound for stuffing mattresses. Horns and hooves sold for anything from $6 to $30 a ton to be converted into buttons, combs and glue.

Nearly all trace of one of the greatest terrestrial biomasses in the history of the earth had vanished, or almost vanished. By 1903 it was reckoned that there were just 21 wild buffalo left, 21 out of a probable

60 million. As far as the general public was concerned the loss of 60 million buffalo meant nothing at all. They were too remote from it to feel any guilt. The same went for America's politicians and industrialists. There were, however, one or two notable exceptions, the most important of whom was later to become President.

The Great Slaughter was being repeated on the other side of the Atlantic in southern Africa. There a similar kind of human migration was taking place, this time northwards instead of to the west. The Voortrekkers with their families packed into ox wagons sought the same kind of life that had driven the American pioneers towards the Rockies and beyond. The Voortrekkers carried a Bible in one hand and a rifle in the other.* They were dead shots as the British soldier was to find out later when he fought the Boers. As the Voortrekkers crossed the Low Veldt of the Orange Free State and the Transvaal, they found themselves surrounded by a golden sea of antelope, most of which were springbok. At least 40 million of these little, gazelle-like antelope inhabited the Low Veldt at that time. Like the buffalo, it seemed their numbers could never be diminished. As with the buffalo, the hunters were coming.

We have an eye-witness account of the springbok throngs from George Gordon Cumming, son of a Scottish baronet, wild man and true eccentric who, like many hunter adventurers of his day, took an army commission largely as a means of finding sport with horse and gun. In fact, he took three commissions until he found one to his liking, in South Africa's Cape Mounted Rifles. Roualeyn Gordon Cumming, to give him his full name, hunted mainly from horseback and always in a kilt. Against the advice of more experienced friends at the Cape, he decided in 1844 to make a personal 12-month trek into the interior with a positive armoury of weapons and ammunition. He found that he got on quite well with the Boers who, he wrote, 'are rather partial to Scotchmen [sic] but detest the sight of an Englishman.' Eccentric and show-off he may have been but he was an experienced hunter and excellent observer of the natural scene, so there is no reason to doubt his account of the springbok migration that he met early on in his trek.

---

* Much of the early slaughter was made with the *roer* fired from horseback. This flintlock rifle was smooth-bored and long enough in the barrel to clear the pony's ears. It fired solid balls and when loaded tightly enough was accurate up to 200 yards. Later came the *sterloop*, made in Birmingham around 1842, and firing a 12-bore ball. The *sterloop* accounted for most of the great game herds.

This was, I think, the most extraordinary and striking scene, as connected with the beasts of the chase, that I ever beheld. For about two hours before the day dawned I had been lying awake in my wagon listening to the grunting of the bucks within two hundred yards of me, imagining that some large herd of springbok was feeding beside my camp. But on rising when it was clear and looking about me I beheld the ground to the northward of my camp actually covered by a dense living mass of springboks, marching slowly and steadily along and extending from an opening in a long range of hills to the west, through which they continued pouring like the flood of some great river, about a mile to the north-east over which they disappeared. The breadth of the ground they covered might have been somewhere about half a mile. I stood upon the fore-chest of my wagon for about two hours, lost in wonder at the novel and wonderful scene which was passing before me and had some difficulty convincing myself that it was reality which I beheld and not the wild and exaggerated picture of a hunter's dream. During this time, vast legions continued streaming through the neck of the hills in one unbroken compact phalanx.

Finally it was, of course, too much for him. 'At length I saddled up and rode into the midst of them with my rifle and after-riders and fired into the ranks until 14 had fallen when I cried "enough." We then retraced our steps to secure the venison which lay strewed along my gory track.' Later the same day: 'On clearing the low range of hills through which the springboks had been pouring, I beheld the boundless plains and even the hillsides which stretched away on every side of me, thickly covered and not with single herds but with one vast herd of springboks; as far as the eye could strain the landscape was alive with them, until they softened down into a dim red mass of living creatures.'

The springbok were mainly grazers which would compete with the settlers' stock. Boer rifles made short work of most of them. They made even shorter work of the scarcer antelope like the blesbok, the bontebok and the zebra-related quagga. The quagga disappeared forever and the bontebok nearly followed. Thanks to a painstaking breeding programme, the surviving bontebok held on in small numbers in Cape Point Reserve, Cape Province. The decimated springbok must be content with the ironic fact that they became their country's national emblem. Today, they can be seen in something like their former glory only in Etosha National Park, Namibia.

As in the case of the American buffalo, some good was to come, almost too late, of this great massacre. It had awakened the conscience of a few powerful and forward-looking men.

*

The Great Slaughter was not confined to land animals. For one victim of this wildlife pogrom, the passenger pigeon of North America, the solution *was* final. In 1813, the great bird artist, John James Audubon, estimated that he had watched a billion of these small, long-tailed pigeons fly over on migration and that this was only a small fraction of the total population. As a wildlife artist, Audubon was an acute observer of nature. He was also a backwoodsman and a hunter so it is unlikely that he overstated the case. In fact, he recorded each flock with a dot in his notebook as they passed.

A quarter of a century later, the last survivor of this enormous throng died in Cincinnnati Zoo. So momentous was this moment of extinction that not only the day but the hour and minute at which the last of the species died have also been recorded:

1 September 1914, 1 pm.

Extinction at such a rate is almost unimaginable, even when you allow for the reception that awaited the birds in their nightly roosting woods. We have Audubon's own account of this.

As the time of their arrival approached, their foes anxiously prepared to receive them. Some persons were ready with iron pots containing sulphur, others with torches of pine knots: many had poles and the rest, guns ...

As the birds arrived and passed over me I felt a current of air that surprised me. Thousands of pigeons were knocked down by the pole men, while more continued to pour in. The fires were lighted and then a magnificent, wonderful and almost terrifying sight presented itself.

The pigeons, arriving by thousands, alighted everywhere, one above the other, until solid masses were formed on the branches all around. The perches gave way under their weight and fell to the ground destroying hundreds of birds underneath ... I found it quite useless to speak or even shout to those persons nearest to me. Even the gun reports were seldom heard ...

Next morning, when the hunters had gathered up all they could possibly use or dispose of, the hogs were driven in to feed on the piles of birds that remained. Audubon noted that he could hardly imagine that even killing on this scale could put an end to so numerous a species. He wrote: 'I have satisfied myself by long observation that nothing but a gradual diminution of our forests can accomplish their decrease.'

Audubon was well before his time in recognising as a prime factor in species destruction the disastrous effect of environmental change. The cutting down of nesting trees by settlers played a large part in the passenger pigeon's disappearance. Successful reproduction seems to have depended on there being enough birds in a flock to provide the necessary social and breeding stimulus.

*

At sea the Great Slaughter had begun earlier than elsewhere. The sea otter of the Northern Pacific carries some of the richest fur in the world. By the end of the eighteenth century, the Russian fur hunters had killed half a million sea otters around the coast of Alaska. When this stock was exhausted, they turned south to California where the otters thrived in the kelp beds as far south at Monterey. The Americans joined them in the hunt. Together the traders built Fort Ross, 240 miles north of San Francisco, as a base for their operations. By 1841, the Californian otters had gone the same way as those further north. The Russians not only abandoned Fort Ross but saw no further use for Alaska once the otter trade had collapsed. In 1867, the Russians sold Alaska to the United States for $7 million, one of the greatest bargains in history. In fact, neither the Russians nor the Americans had killed the last sea otter, but it was not until 1938 that a road gang working on the California highway spotted a concentration of otters in the kelp beds near Monterey. That population is now thriving. Otters have also re-established themselves on the Alaskan coast.

*

The Northern Pacific was also the killing ground for another fur-bearing marine mammal, the northern race of the fur seal. The Pribilof Islands in the Bering Sea, some 350 miles north of the Aleutian Chain were the scene of this great slaughter. Such was the wholesale destruction by Japanese, Russian, British and American sealers that by the end of the last century the fur seal was in danger of being wiped out. In 1911, the four sealing nations drew up a convention to stop hunting. Left undisturbed, seals are prolific breeders. Their population quickly recovered and even permitted the harvesting of surplus males by the US Fish and Wildlife Service.*

There is a lesson in the fur seal story for saving other marine mammals, notably what is left of the world's great whales. It is that if you declare a moratorium on hunting an endangered marine species and provided – it is a big 'if' – its habitat and food supply remain intact, you may, after a long enough interval, be able to start taking a reasonable harvest again. Of course, there is always the likelihood that by that time such a kill may not be desirable, ethical or economically necessary.

During the years of the Great Slaughter, the whalers were even less inclined to take notice of this doctrine than are some of the whaling nations today. Probably, like the buffalo hunters and passenger pigeon killers they simply did not believe that they were running down an apparently endless resource. At the height of the New England whaling industry, between 1835 and 1860, there were some 700 vessels operating out of Boston, Newport and New Bedford. Other whaling nations added about 200 more catchers to the world fleet of hunters. In that period, these ships virtually shot the sperm whale, bowhead and right whale out of north Atlantic and Pacific waters. They then roamed as far as the Indian Ocean and Hawaii. The American whalers stayed at sea for as long as five years until their holds were filled with oil and their decks stacked high with whale bone. In one ten-year period, American whalers brought in 41,241,310 gallons of sperm whale oil alone.

By 1880, a British whaling captain reported that the sperm whale grounds off the Galapagos Islands, 600 miles out in the Pacific from the coast of Ecuador, were 'dry cruising'. Even there the whales had been slaughtered to such an extent that the long voyage was no longer economically worthwhile. And in all this it has to be remembered that the hunt was conducted under sail and the kill made from whale-boats manned and propelled by muscle power. Harpoons were hurled by the same force and at considerable risk to the thrower and the boat's crew. In a three-year voyage, a whaler of the period might kill fewer than 40 whales, about one a month. It can fairly be said that a modern catcher is capable of killing 30 times as many whales in the same period.

---

* In 1972 hunting was stopped. The Pribilof fur seal population had mysteriously started to fall again but not through hunting this time. The most probable cause seemed to be over-fishing of the seals' prey species. In addition, large numbers were known to have been drowned in nylon fishing nets.

Proportionately, and taking into account the means of hunting at their disposal, those nineteenth-century whalers earned themselves a prominent place in the sorry record of mankind during the years of the Great Slaughter.

It is my belief that when mankind's conscience at last stirred it was as a direct reaction to the mass animal murder committed during those terrible years. It was already late in the day. For some species it was too late. But the first moves towards conservation of wildlife were about to be made.

2

The Twinge of Conscience

Despite the millions of animals that had been killed during the years of the Great Slaughter, it was the desire to save the landscape rather than wildlife that provoked the first great act of conservation. Nowadays it is basic to conservation that if you wish to save wild animals you must first save and protect their habitat. When the Americans set up the world's first national park, wildlife wasn't their prime consideration. Laudable as their aims were, they were intent on protecting the beauty rather than the beast.

On 30 January 1872, President Ulysses S. Grant signed a bill that created Yellowstone, not only the first national park in America but the first national park in the world. It is unlikely that the President was moved primarily by the plight of the nearly-vanished buffalo. The Indian wars still had some time to rage, and, as a victorious general of the Civil War, Grant undoubtedly saw the military logic of depriving the plains Indians of their commissariat. Equally there is no doubt that the President, who had witnessed so much destruction, saw the need to preserve the scenic wonders of his country before they too were destroyed, or at least despoiled, by the westward tide of development and industrialisation.

Yellowstone is so important as a conservation landmark that the history of how it became the first national park has to be told in some detail. The mountain men, the beaver trappers, knew all about the wonders of Yellowstone and probably took them for granted. In 1810, when a trapper called John Colter, and then James Bridger in the 1840s, tried to tell the outside world about Yellowstone, the stories were dismissed as too outrageous to be believed, let alone to print. Once branded a liar, Bridger thought he might just as well justify his reputation and began to embroider a little. He told how he missed a shot at an elk because 'a glass mountain' got in the way. Today tourists stare in wonder at the black obsidian cliff of volcanic glass. Bridger described an icy spring in the mountains that 'gushed forth waters which raced downhill so fast that the river turned warm on the bottom'. Modern visitors wade in the Firestone River and feel the heat from the rocks in its bed. Bridger told of an Indian medicine man who had cursed one area with instant death. What he was really describing were the petrified trees along Specimen Ridge.

'A feller can catch fish in an icy river,' Bridger wrote, 'pull it in a boiling pool and cook his fish without ever taking it off the hook,' – a boast that wasn't so far from the truth.

After Bridger and his fellow trappers came the gold-seekers of 1849. They found no gold in Yellowstone despite the promise of its name. In 1859 a small military expedition entered the future park but didn't get far because of the deep snow. In fact, there are only four and a half months in the year in which it is possible to move about the whole park. The rest of the time, the snow is between 4 and 14 feet deep.

The first expedition to explore the area fully was composed of three residents of the Territory, as it was then called, of Montana. In 1869, the Cook-Fulsom-Peterson Expedition returned with accounts of geysers and hot springs. Their stories were still thought to be wildly exaggerated. An official expedition was sent in the next year to learn the truth. It was official only in as much as it had a military escort of Lieutenant Gustavus C. Doane and four enlisted men. The word of the four principal expedition members was more likely to be accepted. They included: General Henry D. Washburn, Surveyor General of Montana, Cornelius Hedges, a Montana judge, and Nathaniel D. Langford, later to become the superintendent of the world's first national park.

In under four weeks they saw and confirmed all the scenic wonders that John Colter had described sixty years before, James Bridger had enlarged upon and the Cook-Fulsom-Peterson Expedition had reported the previous year. When these men sat round their camp fire at the end of their trek they discussed the future of Yellowstone. Their first notion was to split the area up among themselves since they rightly saw that in the years to come people would pay a great deal to visit Yellowstone. Finally, the judge spoke up and put the proposal that there should be no private ownership of such a miraculous place but that it should be set aside for the enjoyment of all Americans. In an age of get-there-first-and-grab-it this was pretty advanced thinking. To their credit, Judge Hedges' fellow explorers accepted his idea, and a year later, William Clagett, a newly elected congressman from Montana, introduced a bill for a National Park Act in the House of

Representatives. The reward for the members of the Washburn-Langford-Doane Expedition is that each man has a mountain named after him.

*

Twelve years after the creation of Yellowstone National Park, President Kruger of South Africa proposed, with perhaps even greater foresight than that of Grant and the American politicians, to set up a national park. His concern was directly for the wildlife, but then 'Oom Paul' Kruger had been both farmer and hunter.

In 1869, gold was discovered in the Lydenburg district of the Low Veldt and prospectors and adventurers flocked in. The Low Veldt, which had been pretty well left alone until then, became anybody's hunting ground. High Veldt farmers descended the escarpment to find winter grazing for their stock and stayed to hunt. Professionals shot for ivory, horns, skin, trophies and meat. Game numbers declined so rapidly that in 1884, twelve years after the foundation of Yellowstone, President Kruger proposed in the Volksraad that a game sanctuary be established to save the fast disappearing wildlife of the Transvaal. It was not a popular idea among a pioneering, farming people. It took another fourteen years before two quite small areas between the Crocodile and Sabi Rivers were proclaimed protected areas with penalties for destroying, wounding or hunting game. The Sabi and Shingwedsi Reserves were the small beginnings of what was to become, twenty-eight years later, the Kruger National Park.

In the beginning no staff was appointed to look after the reserves, but Police Sergeant Holzhausen, stationed at Komatiport, was told that he must keep an eye open for poachers. In the event, the Boer War broke out exactly a year later and game reserves were forgotten, both sides shooting as much as they wanted to supplement their rations.

After the Peace of Vereeniging in 1902, the interim government under Lord Milner remembered the Sabi Reserve and reinstated it. A Scots regular soldier, Major (later Colonel) James Stevenson-Hamilton was put in charge as warden. The Major was seconded from his regiment for two years but stayed for forty. When he took on the task, game laws existed only on paper and the large animals hardly existed at all. Every major species was not only scarce but the survivors had been shot at so often that they were extremely wild.

Stevenson-Hamilton had been given the vaguest of instructions. The only one he remembered clearly in later years was to 'make myself as unpopular as possible among hunters and poachers'. He set to with a will, earning the nickname among the locals of Skukza, 'the one who

13

changes everything'. In 1904 he obtained control over 10,000 square kilometres north of the Sabi River, largely by persuading private owners and mining companies to see things his way. To maintain control over this enlarged reserve he succeeded in getting himself appointed Native Commissioner, Customs Officer, and Justice of the Peace for the territory. This enabled him to imprison evil-doers, to control illegal trade in horns, skins and tusks and to appoint rangers.

He encountered no lack of opponents. After the First World War there was a general outcry for more agricultural land, a problem that arises time and time again in the story of conservation. Most of the Low Veldters were opposed to an end of hunting and even more to being denied areas of pasture and farmland in favour of wild animals. The very existence of the Sabi Reserve seemed threatened. Stevenson-Hamilton realised that the only hope for his sanctuary was to have it proclaimed, like Yellowstone, a national park. He made good political progress on this front until a change of government looked as if it would destroy all his hopes. Fortunately, he won the confidence and support of the new Minister for Lands, P. J. Grobler, who luckily happened to be a nephew of the late and great President Kruger. On 31 May 1926, the National Park Act was passed unanimously, adding many hectares of land north of the Sabi River to the original Sabi Reserve. The whole would henceforth be known as the Kruger National Park. It was only the beginning. In the next decade nine more parks were set up by the South African government.

The lesson of both Yellowstone and Kruger, one founded primarily to protect scenery the other to save wild animals, is that conservation, then as now, depends largely on having the right politicians on the right side at the right time.

*

If one politician deserves to be singled out for right-mindedness in the period immediately following the years of the Great Slaughter, without any doubt it must be Theodore Roosevelt. If some do not look upon him these days as the founding father of national conservation it is because he was that unforgivable thing in many animal-lovers' eyes, a hunter. Yet such an understandable viewpoint overlooks the fact that the true hunter realises better than most that his prey and its habitat must be protected if he is to be able to continue hunting. Beyond this, he usually has a great respect for and understanding of his quarry – this was most certainly the case with Roosevelt who loved both wildlife and the wilderness.

Teddy Roosevelt was born in 1858, the eldest son of a rich New York family of Dutch descent. He grew up in the years in which not only was the buffalo disappearing from the plains but also the industrialisation of the United States was accelerating often at the expense of what would later come to be called the environment. In stature and outlook, Roosevelt was a man as large as, and often larger than, life. He was an immensely physical as well as an intellectual man, and was renowned at Harvard for his skill as a boxer. In the American war with Spain in 1897 he joined a cavalry regiment called the Rough Riders and led a successful unmounted charge to capture an enemy strongpoint at the battle of San Juan Hill. It was no coincidence that he elected to join the Rough Riders in which many of his fellow cavalrymen were former cowhands, for Roosevelt spent as much time as he could spare riding the range with cowboys in Montana. The wilderness was a second home to him. Above all he loved hunting the still abundant big game of the United States – the grizzly, the cougar, the pecary and even the wolf. His first book *The Wilderness Hunter*, published in 1906, showed clearly that he held strong conservationist views.

It is entirely within our power as a nation to preserve large stretches of wilderness which are valueless for agricultural purposes and unfit for settlement as playgrounds for rich and poor alike and to preserve the game so that it shall continue to exist for the benefit of all lovers of nature and to give reasonable opportunities for the exercise of the skills of the hunter whether he is or is not a man of means. But this end can only be achieved by wise laws and resolute enforcement of the laws. Lack of such legislation and administration will result in harm to us all.

Though in his late twenties Roosevelt had hunted buffalo, there is little doubt it was the extermination of the great herds that drove him, first as a private citizen and later as a politician, to promote measures to preserve America's wildlife and wild places. Yellowstone's herd of 200 buffalo was shrinking fast under lax federal protection. Though regulations forbade killing the buffalo in the newly created national park, punishments were derisory, usually the confiscation of hunting equipment and expulsion from the park after which the poacher simply bought a new rifle and returned by another route. In 1893, poachers killed 116 buffalo. Teddy Roosevelt's voice had been at its loudest among politicians demanding action and, in 1894, President Grover Cleveland put his signature to the Lacey Act forbidding the killing of buffalo under penalty of $1,000 fine or imprisonment. It was the first effective protection the federal government had given the buffalo and, of course, it came far too late to stop the rot. By the first year of Roosevelt's presidency the Yellowstone herd had dropped to 25 animals.

Roosevelt entered politics soon after graduating from Harvard in 1880. He became Vice-president under McKinley in 1900. A year later, after McKinley's assassination, he found himself in the White House. If the presidency did not always give Roosevelt the absolute power he needed to enforce some of his conservation measures, he ignored the fact and went ahead just the same. Few people were in a position to argue with Roosevelt in the driving seat, or perhaps saddle. The building of the Panama Canal is usually said to be the greatest contribution to the future made during his administration. Some environmentalists would contest this, claiming that the start he gave to conservation in the USA was his greatest legacy to posterity.

He began in 1903 with a typical grand, swashbuckling gesture. A small island, just offshore from the village of Sebastian in Florida, was a nesting ground for the brown pelican, a bird much persecuted by visiting Palm Beach 'sportsmen' who shot from the decks of passing yachts just for the pleasure of seeing the birds fall. The American Ornithologists' Union had tried to buy the island but discovered that it was what was known as 'unsurveyed government property'. The fact that the ornithologists had been thwarted by government ownership of the island found its way to the President's desk, where Roosevelt provided an easy solution. Though his advisers told him he would be overstepping his authority if he decided to make the island into a bird refuge – there was no precedent for such action – Roosevelt simply dictated a document and signed it.

It is hereby ordered that Pelican Island in Indian River in Section Nine, Township Thirty One South, Range Thirty Nine East, State of Florida, be, and it is hereby reserved and set apart for the use of the Department of Agriculture as a preserve and breeding ground for native birds.   (Theodore Roosevelt. March 14, 1903)

Roosevelt had started something tremendous, for Pelican Island became the first National Wildlife Refuge. There are today 477 such refuges, ranging from Alaska to Key Deer off the southernmost tip of Florida. They protect a whole range of American fauna from the pronghorn antelope to the snow goose and cover 90 million acres. Then in 1905, by an executive order, Roosevelt created a large reserve on US Forestry Service lands in Oklahoma's Wichita Territory. Conservationists led by men like Dr Hornaday, first director of the

New York Zoological Park and one of the founders of the American Bison Society, pressurised Congress to allot $15,000 to build a 7½ foot-high buffalo-proof fence around 8,000 acres of the Wichita Refuge. On 11 October 1907, 15 of the finest buffalo selected from the New York Zoological Park were taken by rail to the small town of Cache, Oklahoma in two luxury horse transportation rail cars. There, before an audience of cowhands and Comanche Indians, they were released into the fenced area. It is recorded that the Indians, who included the venerable chief Quanah Parker, the last great leader of the Comanches, wept as they saw the buffalo on which their people had once depended returning to the prairie.

This was perhaps the first instance of reintroduction on a large scale, and better than anything, it demonstrated Roosevelt's foresight. Today Wichita Mountains National Wildlife Refuge, the second in the system which Roosevelt created at Pelican Island with the stroke of a pen, encloses around 60,000 acres and is encircled by 95 miles of big game fence. The original 15 animals prospered. Their offspring have been translocated to start many other herds. Before his administration came to an end in 1909, Roosevelt played a large political part in setting up more buffalo refuges, as a result of which the present bison population of the USA is of the order of 15,000 animals.

When he left office, Roosevelt made a long hunting safari in East Africa with his son Kermit. Many photos of this trip exist, most of them showing the great man with his foot metaphorically, if not actually, on a fallen big game animal. In all, the presidential party killed 9 lions, 5 hyenas, 8 elephants, 13 rhinos, 7 hippos, and 6 Cape buffalo. Roosevelt noted in his diary: '296 head, self; Kermit, 216 head; we did not kill a hundredth part of what we could have done.' They did, however, kill 9 white rhinos, well over the permitted limit for an animal easy to shoot even in earlier days when hunters used muzzle-loading rifles.

It is a pity that for many the memory of this hunting safari obliterates the pioneering work that Teddy Roosevelt did for conservation in his own country. As a hunter of his time he saw nothing excessive in what he did in a land like East Africa, where game was still so plentiful. No doubt he expected others to view things in the same light. Despite being progressive in many ways, Roosevelt was subject to the limited view of his time. In the century in which Roosevelt was born, the great bell tolled for millions upon millions of wild animals. At the beginning of the century in which he died, a far smaller bell had started to ring for conservation. It is fair to say that Theodore Roosevelt's hand was the principal one that tugged the bell rope.

3

Cull for Kindness

At first saving wild animals seemed simple. You found a large tract of wilderness, an area of great natural beauty and preferably one that no one else had any use for, gazetted it as a reserve, made some laws to protect its flora and fauna, and looked upon that as a job well done. With average good fortune, the animals inside it would prosper, as would the vegetation. Unfortunately conservation turned out to be a good deal more complicated than that.

The United States followed Yellowstone by protecting a whole series of its natural wonders. These areas had to be supervised, even policed, to keep poachers under control. But who was to do the job? No specialist ranger force existed. The army seemed the obvious solution so, in 1886, it took over the running of Yellowstone. With a whole new string of parks to look after, the government soon realised that the army wasn't right for the job. In 1916 Congress created a National Parks Service which appointed superintendents and rangers and set the pattern which most national parks use to this day.

One ingredient that was later to prove vital was missing – science. At the time there was no apparent need to seek the advice of wildlife biologists, even had such experts existed. As to the word 'ecology', few would have known what it meant. To protect wilderness was enough. In that early heyday, conservation was largely a seat-of-the-pants operation. Superintendents and rangers were mainly instinctive naturalists who had learned about wildlife in the mountains, deserts and backwoods, many of them as hunters – not that they were any the worse at their jobs for that. The day when scientists would tell them how they should provide for and look after their wild charges was long distant. The problems which those scientists would be called in to solve had yet to emerge; the man-pressure which would soon squeeze all wildlife situations had not yet been fully applied.

In the early 1800s up to 60 million wild buffalo roamed the prairies of North America; by 1903, there were just 21 left.

The railroad companies of Kansas ran cheap buffalo-hunting trips by train. Carcases were left by the track to rot.

Tranquillising drugs were so unreliable in 1961 that Uganda's remaining white rhinos had to be captured by lasso. They were all later killed by poachers.

By the mid-1970s immobilising techniques had improved dramatically. Using a crossbow, Nick Carter darts Ugandan black rhinos.

Since national parks, national refuges and reserves were later to form the fortress in which wildlife would eventually make its stand, arguably its very last stand, it is important to consider how and where such protected areas first evolved. Once the pioneering work had been done in America and South Africa, governments elsewhere began to get the idea that setting up parks and refuges was not only public-spirited and necessary but was also inexpensive. The idea caught on like a bush fire. All you had to do, it seemed, was to light the green touch paper.

Europe was a different and more difficult proposition. The history of land use there was well-established: most land belonged to royalty, the Church, private land-owners or industry. Even by the First World War, there was little wilderness not already spoken for. Much of the remainder which was sufficiently remote or unsuitable for economic development lay in Scandinavia. In 1909, Sweden created the first European national park in Lapland, at Abisko, Stora Sjofallet and Lepjekaise. Two more parks at Sarek and Sonfjallet followed shortly afterwards.

Switzerland established the first alpine national park near Zernez in 1914. It was founded on the principle – prescient in view of what was to come elsewhere – of non-interference with nature. The idea was to let plants and animals solve their own problems. No extra feed would be put down for chamois or ibex in winter. If they couldn't forage for themselves, they would starve. No forestry would be carried out. Trees would live out their lives, fall and die, creating their own tangle of undergrowth, promoting their own regeneration. Even at that time, before the problems affecting reserves and parks had begun to make themselves felt, naturalists were sceptical about this leave-it-all-to-mother-nature philosophy. Amazingly, the alpine park flourished, undoubtedly because the mountains contained their own eco-system adjusted to an environment that is kind enough in spring and summer and harsh enough in winter to keep flora and fauna in balance – provided man does not intervene in the system.

Spain acted next, in 1918, with Covadonga in the Cantabrian Mountains and then the great canyon of Ordesa in the Pyrenees. These early southern European parks met with little opposition. The land was either useless for agriculture or had traditionally been shared as grazing by both wild animals and domestic stock. The locals, therefore, accepted the new parks, where administration and policing by rangers either did not exist or was not strong enough to curtail the little hunting the resident humans had always carried out.

Such tolerance was unlikely to last. In his book *National Parks of Western Europe*, Angus Waycott writes: 'Landowners naturally regarded with suspicion any encroachment on the principle of unrestricted land use and early conservationists were quick to realise that a successful (though expensive) way to overcome their opposition was to buy them out.' To do this, organisations like the British National Trust (1895) were formed all over Europe to raise money from private and government sources to preserve places of special beauty.

One more European national park merits special mention. The Gran Paradiso in the Italian Alps was the first park set up primarily with the aim of saving an individual species – the alpine ibex, the large mountain goat whose males carry enormous back-swept horns. By the 1800s the ibex had been hunted almost out of existence. It was given protection in 1821 and began to recover its numbers well. Thirty-five years later, the Gran Paradiso became a royal hunting preserve, with the result that such predators as the wolf and the lynx were shot out. It was a pattern that was later to be repeated in many other parks. Once the predators had been exterminated or at least greatly reduced, the ecology of the reserve was knocked out of natural balance and the ibex ceased to disperse so widely, with the result that they not only over-grazed their range but became far too inbred. Disease and illegal hunting did the rest. By the First World War extinction seemed certain. Then, in 1922, the king of Italy, Victor Emmanuel, renounced his royal hunting rights and declared the Gran Paradiso a national park in which the natural balance was to be restored by good management as soon as possible. The ibex has since flourished, and animals have been taken from the park to stock other mountain areas.

Today every major country has its national parks. For emergent nations, which gained independence in the 1950s and 1960s, having national parks was almost as important as running a national airline. Parks became a matter of prestige and an outward sign of progress and civilization, even if some contained few animals. Some countries were able to designate huge areas in this way. Designation is the easy part. Equipping such parks with wardens costs a lot of money that is often unavailable. At the very least such gestures can be looked upon as a step in the right direction.

★

For most people, the words national park conjure up a picture of one continent only – Africa. Africa is a huge land mass over much of which – though increasingly less – wild animals still roam, sometimes, as in the case of the Serengeti in Tanzania, in millions. So it is natural that much of the work directed at studying and saving wildlife should be concentrated there. No African national parks typify the whole visionary, heroic and sometimes tragic conservation story more than the two original parks of Uganda, Murchison Falls (now Kabalega) National Park and the Queen Elizabeth (now Ruwenzori) National Park.

The creation of the Ugandan parks was fairly similar to what was taking place just after the Second World War in other African countries still under colonial rule. In all these, the setting up of parks was a white enterprise. Very few, if any, Africans, let alone their future politicians, saw the need to protect wildlife, nor indeed did Africans at any level of tribal society have a liking or regard for wild animals. Elephants were a nuisance that destroyed the villagers' meagre crops. Hippos were highly dangerous creatures that ambushed and killed wives going to draw water or wash clothes in the river. Perhaps the only Africans who had a true respect for wild animals were those who lived by hunting.

In Uganda's case, the driving force for the establishment of national parks was the then Attorney General, Ralph Dreschfield. Such men of wildlife vision existed throughout colonial Africa. In Kenya, his counterpart was Mervyn Cowie, the architect behind the gazetting in December, 1946, of Nairobi National Park. Unlike Cowie, Dreschfield himself was not all that keen on wildlife. He was, however, passionately interested in the future development of Uganda as an independent African nation. He saw parks as natural assets in a country that did not have much else to offer the world.

The Ugandan government proposed an annual grant of £50,000 towards running the parks that Dreschfield envisaged. When critics asked: 'But how are you going to pay for it all?' Dreschfield replied in a written answer:

National parks are not commercial enterprises. They are a service financed by state funds and run for the benefit of the people of the state. Our duty is to provide parks for the recreation of the people of the country. Parks are not and can never be commercial propositions.

Visitors will come from all over the world and when they come they will bring money to the country and so, although the state as such may have to provide money for their upkeep, I have little doubt that indirectly, and I would emphasise that word, our parks will pay for themselves many times over.

To set up the Ugandan parks, Dreschfield appointed a remarkable man called Ken Beaton, who was then working for the national parks of Kenya. Beaton died tragically early but not before he had chosen two wonderful sites for his first Ugandan parks. In the south Queen

Elizabeth National Park looks out to the west over Lake Edward (now Lake Idi Amin) towards the former Belgian Congo (now Zaire). Northward it faces the Ruwenzori, Ptolemy's 'Mountains of the Moon'. It includes the Kazinga Channel, linking lakes Edward and George and contains the magically-named forest, the Maramagambo running down to the Zaire border in the south at Ishasha. When Beaton surveyed it, the area was rich in elephants and over-rich in hippos, perhaps as many as 30,000 of the latter. He guessed that the hippos were consuming the grass that other animals needed and might have to be heavily culled. The savannahs, dotted with stands of euphorbia cactus, were pock-marked with explosion craters from long-past vulcanism. It was in every way a wildlife and scenic paradise. The only fly in the ointment at the time was that it also contained several fishing villages. Resident people and parks do not mix well but this was something that had to be literally lived with. It contained a second fly, the tsetse, of which much more in a moment.

The other park, 300 miles to the north, is even more beautiful. In part it lay in the tribal lands of the Acholi who, being hunters, were natural material for adaptation to wildlife protection and were to provide almost the entire ranger staff of both parks. The other section lay in Bunyoro, the land of the once legendary guerilla warrior chief, Kabarega, who successfully fought rival tribes, tried to wipe out Sir Samuel Baker's expedition in 1874 and defied the British in Uganda until he was finally defeated in 1899 and exiled to the Seychelles islands.

The two tribal lands inside Murchison Falls Park were divided by the Victoria Nile, the river which Samuel Baker reached shortly after John Hanning Speke had found the source of the Nile at Ripon Falls on Lake Victoria. Baker established that his river connected Lake Victoria with his own great discovery Lake Albert. On the Victoria Nile, running through Beaton's proposed park, was the great waterfall which Baker named after the President of the Royal Society, Sir Henry Murchison. At Murchison Falls, the entire river leaps through a chasm barely 20 feet wide and crashes into a great whirlpool 150 feet below. No park could hope for a more spectacular setting.

As to game, Murchison contained at least 5,000 of some of the most magnificent elephants in Africa. The wildlife problems were matters for the future, and they were easily discernible to Beaton's experienced eye. Around the Kazinga Channel in the Queen Elizabeth Park hippos were fast degrading the habitat at the expense of other herbivores. In Murchison, the great armoured divisions of elephants rolled over the woodland like a panzer army, stripping and destroying the trees.

Beaton's assessment of these problems was typical of the time and the sort of man he was, a practical naturalist with a hunter's eye. He estimated (in fact vastly under-estimated) the Murchison elephant population at 2,500 and thought that the seasonal migratory habits of the herds would take them out of the park and thus relieve the pressure on the trees. He foresaw the damage the hippo might do 'if they continue to increase' but added with considerable wisdom that the tons of manure they dropped in the water vastly benefitted the fish stocks of the Kazinga Channel and Lake Edward. He was, however, totally wrong when he wrote: 'fine waterbuck are well distributed and plentiful. Uganda kob are numerous in certain areas as are bushbuck and reedbuck. Wild dog are probably now their greatest enemy and these brutes are to be shot wherever they are encountered.' The scientists who followed in Uganda, and elsewhere in Central Africa, were soon to correct these very natural lay assumptions and to show the wild hunting dogs' value to the antelopes' ecology. It was the ibex and Gran Paradiso story all over again.

Dreschfield and Beaton were men of vision who brought these magnificent parks into being. They were not to know that their great work was later to be almost totally destroyed by the dreadful regime of Idi Amin and the civil wars that followed.

Dreschfield's and Beaton's immediate task was to sell the idea of setting aside such large tracts of country for wild animals in a shortly-to-become-independent African state. They had not only to persuade the existing British colonial administration but also the up-and-coming African politicians soon to take over. Fortunately, they understood public relations. They chartered a Dakota aircraft to take African politicians and journalists on a preview of their proposed parks. In the case of the Queen Elizabeth Park they converted the local ruler, the King of Toro, so completely that he subsequently referred to it as 'my park'. Previously there had been no need for public relations work by conservationists. Later it was to prove essential.

The task of setting up the two Ugandan parks would have been a great deal more difficult, if not impossible, had not both chosen areas been totally unsuitable for ranching or grazing cattle – many African parks owe their existence to this one factor – for both the plains of Queen Elizabeth and the savannahs of Murchison are tsetse fly country. Though these days the fly is seldom a danger to human life, no cow can live with it and tsetse country is therefore useless for livestock farmers. Little does this otherwise tiresome insect realise how much its bite has contributed to saving wildlife in many African countries by 'reserving' large areas of wilderness for wild animals (see Notes on the Tsetse Fly).

National parks are obviously a key step in saving the animals that live within their boundaries. Setting up a national park apparently solves in one move the most important problem of all, giving those animals total protection. Unfortunately creating a park often produces as many wildlife problems as it solves, for no matter how wide the boundaries, the protected area is always an arbitrary and artifical one, and this affects big migratory mammals in particular. Large animals like the elephants, buffalo and elk traditionally move with the seasons to find fresh food and water. The mere fact that some kind authority has given them a large backyard to play in makes no impact on their instinctive behaviour patterns. Elephants, which historically migrate perhaps 200 or 300 miles to avoid the scarcities of the dry season and the dangers of the wet, aren't going to stop just because someone has drawn a line round them designating a national park. Once outside the park they find their age-old routes barred by villages, shambas, roads and railways. They also increasingly find the poachers waiting for them.

Another situation created by the protection a park gives is over-production of some species due to security and at least a temporary abundance of food. The effect is disastrous for several species, including the offenders. There were two classic cases right at the start of the Ugandan parks' lives. In Murchison Falls, the elephants, encouraged to stay within the 1,500-square-mile park by the safety it afforded, systematically took the woodlands apart. Huge stands of acacia and terminalia were ring-barked by elephants, possibly in search of certain minerals they lacked, so that whole woodlands died. Many trees were simply torn out of the ground or pushed over in the elephants' search for food. In earlier years the elephants' needs would have been satisfied by migration. It was a sad outcome of protection that was to be repeated elsewhere.

In the Queen Elizabeth Park in the south of Uganda it was the hippos that caused the trouble. Around the Kazinga Channel the nocturnal wanderings of hippo in search of grass denuded the savannah for hundreds of yards from the banks. There was, moreover, an endless supply of hippos. They not only flourished in the Kazinga Channel but also all round the considerable shoreline of Lake Edward. On the southern shores of the great lake, in the then Belgian Congo, lay the Parc Albert.

The total hippo population of these waters was probably in excess of 30,000. The situation was not helped by the fact that the Belgian scientific director of the Parc Albert, Jacques Verschuren, believed that nature should be left to work out its own problems. If the hippos were putting other herbivores at risk with their greed, then that was the way nature, at the particular moment, saw things. If it went on long enough, the hippos themselves would be hit by lack of food and would suffer a population crash.

This was all very well if your park was sufficiently large to cope with such an evolutionary approach; the Parc Albert was not. Moreover this attitude overlooked the facts that the far smaller Queen Elizabeth Park, whose authorities did not necessarily share Verschuren's theories, was on the receiving end of his surplus hippos, and that parks are for people to enjoy. If the animals they contained greatly decreased through their own depredations, the overseas tourist was far less likely to travel long distances to see them. This would lose the country revenue. Far more important in Dreschfield's and Beaton's eyes was that the African wasn't going to come either, or, if he did, would not be sufficiently impressed to think that parks were worthwhile or enjoyable.

The problem of the Queen Elizabeth Park hippos was one of the first to be tackled on a large scale by a team of scientists. In 1965 the Ugandan parks were offered the services of three Fulbright Scholars. Senator J. William Fulbright, himself a Rhodes Scholar, had proposed that countries which had received wartime lease-lend aid from America should help repay this by funding American scholars on overseas projects. Three Fulbrighters, all animal biologists, were welcomed by Britain and Uganda. They found research projects enough in the Ugandan parks. Dr Petrides of Michigan State University estimated that there were at least 10,000 hippos around the Kazinga Channel alone and that if something was not done to thin them out soon the environment would suffer, possibly beyond repair. His answer was a shocking one: to shoot 3,000 hippos a year for several years and then to keep down the natural increase thereafter. The proposal predictably raised a storm. What would the Trustees of the Parks Board, let alone the visitors, make of such a slaughter? What would be the effect on the African population and on African politicians soon to take over the running of their country? How could wardens and rangers hope to control illegal hunting if they themselves were killing the very animals they were supposed to protect?

It took a year to win the Trustees' agreement. In his Chairman's report, Ralph Dreschfield wrote:

We are satisfied that we have a positive duty to the flora and fauna within our parks and to prosperity to take all the steps which we consider necessary to ensure the survival of that flora and fauna and the survival of the parks as a pleasure and educational ground for the people of the Protectorate, even if carrying out of that duty requires us to destroy some of the flora and fauna.

In April, 1958, the Trustees pushed the button and the shooting began. A new word had been introduced to the management of animals in national parks. It began as 'cropping' but soon became 'culling'.

After the Fulbrighters went home, the work was taken up by the Nuffield Unit for Tropical Animal Ecology (NUTAE) established at Mweya, Queen Elizabeth Park headquarters, under Dick Laws, later to become Director of the British Antarctic Survey. The cull was made respectable, at least in the eyes of science, by the use of the bodies of the shot hippos for research into population dynamics. Once science had, so to speak, had its cut, the meat was given away or sold cheaply for local consumption. Thus nothing was wasted and much necessary knowledge gained. After all, until it was known how fast hippos bred or what proportion of males and females they produced, it was extremely hard to know how many or what gender to kill. Despite the respectability given to the killing by these legitimate means and arguments, there were still many both inside and outside national park organisations who felt that it was contrary to all conservation principles to kill animals instead of saving them. The Fulbrighters and NUTAE scientists and their supporters argued that, in the long run, this was exactly what they were doing.

Before long the same treatment on a more limited scale was being given to a far smaller number of Murchison Falls elephants. There, too, research as well as population reduction (aimed at saving the woodlands) were the guiding principles. It was thought kinder to obliterate whole family herds. Elephants are a matriarchal society in which mothers, sisters, aunts, female cousins and young of both sexes are all dependent on each other. Bulls are relatively unimportant. They simply visit the herds to impregnate in-season females. It was argued by NUTAE, and later generally accepted, that to kill half a cow herd would leave the remainder disoriented and possibly leaderless. A kill by kindness therefore, had to be a total kill. It was a tragedy whichever way you looked at it and not the sort of thing the tourists should to know about. So the culling was done in a little-visited part of the park well off the recognised tracks. No-one could have foretold how ironic the culling would turn out to be. Almost the entire elephant population of the park was to be slaughtered during the bloody and terrible days of Idi Amin's misrule.

There was a further irony in the whole national parks' rationale. Apart from being set up to protect their wildlife inmates, national parks were created for people to visit and enjoy. Very soon it became clear that the visitor was as much part of the park's ecology as its flora and fauna. The smaller the park, the greater the tourists' impact, usually destructive, on its environment. If you are dealing with a park like Etosha in Namibia – one third the size of Switzerland – you can afford to sectionalise it, or, to use the jargon word, 'zone' it. Zoning means that one third, say, is open to tourists, one third left totally untouched and one third reserved for scientific research. At the other extreme are small parks like Amboseli in Kenya, ideal for game-viewing. Amboseli contains a large population of animals and is well served by vehicle tracks and tourist lodges. The animals are attracted to it and held almost all the year round by two large swamps which are fed by water from springs that originate in streams running down from the lava slopes of Mount Kilimanjaro, a magnificent backdrop to the park. The park is a 'must' on the safari circuit run by tour companies operating out of Nairobi. Its soil is salty, white and powdery. Much of it began life deep inside the earth until the erupting Kilimanjaro spewed it out millions of years ago. The zebra-striped buses pound round the tracks with their guided loads of tourists in search of lion on a kill or giraffe feeding from the tops of acacia trees. In pursuit of this entirely legitimate exercise, their wheels churn up huge clouds of white dust that settle on every living thing. The wear and tear on Amboseli's environment is continuous and extensive.

In an imperfect world in which the wilderness is continually shrinking, no one has so far come up with a better solution for both protecting wildlife and making it accessible to the public. It is unlikely that anyone ever will. It would be far preferable, of course, if large chunks of the remaining wilderness could be left untouched and undeveloped. So long as there is a chance of someone making a fast buck by finding oil in the wilderness, grazing more cattle there or by chopping down trees to make charcoal or building material, then this is unlikely ever to happen. So the establishment of national parks and reserves, whatever their problems and drawbacks, remains the best and perhaps the only answer.

4

Smash and Grab

In the short history of conservation, one decade stands out – the 1950s, when many African national parks came into being and mankind, recovering from the Second World War, had time to think of something other than its own survival. One of the events that gave conservation an impetus was in itself a wildlife disaster. This happening possibly did more to focus the world's attention on the plight of wildlife in developing countries than any single event before or since. It took place on the borders of two game reserves and affected a huge area of African bush around a place known as Kariba.

A decision was taken by the governments of Northern and Southern Rhodesia, together with the Federal government (the Federation then included the two Rhodesias and Nyasaland) to hold back the waters of the Zambesi River at Kariba with a great dam. The dam would not only supply power for the copper belt, it would create behind its walls an immense lake which, stocked with fish, especially tilapia, a highly palatable food fish, would eventually allow an annual catch of 9,000 tonnes.

Apart from engineering considerations, an enormous amount of planning preceded this enterprise. Fifty thousand Tonga tribesmen had to be resettled at a cost of £4 million. Schemes were drawn up for three new townships on each side of the lake. In all this organisation, only one factor was left unconsidered – the fate of the flora and fauna. Ignoring the appeals of their respective game departments, the governments of the two Rhodesias went ahead. The bulldozers moved in dragging ships' anchor chains to which were attached 8-foot steel balls. Only the giant baobab trees offered the slightest resistance to the clearance of bush at the rate of 50 acres an hour. Some 100,000 acres were due to be cleared in all, to provide fishing grounds where nets would not snag on underwater obstructions as well as harbours for an industry which would eventually feed thousands of people. Tilapia fingerlings bred at the Northern Rhodesia Game and Fisheries Department near Lusaka, now the capital of Zambia, were put into the lake at the rate of 10 tonnes per year.

Early in December 1958 the great wall at Kariba was sealed behind its protective coffer dam. The effects were almost immediate. For 50 miles downstream of the dam, to the point at which Kafue River joins it, the Zambesi was reduced to a twentieth of its normal dry season flow. Wildlife, to which the river had previously been an impassable barrier, could now cross. Normally this would not have mattered since both banks were infested with tsetse fly. However, only on the southern bank were the trypanosomes that carried human sleeping sickness present. No-one had, of course, seen this side-effect of damming the river. Panic action followed. A cordon of game guards was established on both banks to try to prevent the interchange of animals. Thunderflashes were used in an attempt to drive back animals in whose bloodstream might be the 'tryps' potentially deadly to humans. When all else failed, many animals were shot.

Above the dam, thousands of tiger fish were found dead on the surface of the rapidly rising lake. Tiger fish are not good to eat but they are greatly valued by sport anglers. The manner of the tiger fishes' death was a further illustration of the innumerable and often damaging consequences which follow when man interferes with nature without asking the right questions first. The tiger fish had died as the result of eating a surfeit of crickets which the rising waters had driven from their holes in the banks!

Much worse was to follow. High ground cut off by the lake became islands which rapidly grew smaller and smaller. The game animals that had taken refuge on these had no way of knowing that they were marooned and that they would eventually eat all the available food and starve to death – if they were not drowned first.

At first no move was made by the Northern Rhodesian government. Someone even suggested that there was no need to mount a rescue operation as the animals could probably be driven to higher ground. This was tried but it was a complete failure. In Southern Rhodesia, four game rangers under the leadership of an intrepid man called Rupert Fothergill began a rescue attempt.

In February 1959, the Rhodesian press picked up the story and began to play it up strongly. Aitken Cade, leader of the opposition in the Southern Rhodesian Parliament, tabled a private motion that: 'in the opinion of this house, the rescue methods adopted by the government have been, and still are inadequate'. The resolution had its effect,

Mr Cade cancelled his motion when the government responded by greatly increasing its aid. Northern Rhodesia still dragged its feet. The government there proposed a reconnaissance of the islands to assess the size of the problem and agreed to consider an offer by the Game Preservation and Hunting Association to mobilise its members as rescue workers. It was another example of the hunters taking a lead in conservation, only partly from self-interest.

By March it was obvious that the Northern Rhodesian government intended to do very little. The Game Preservation and Hunting Association decided to ask for help from the Fauna Preservation Society in London. The Society (now the Fauna and Flora Preservation Society) responded at once and called a press conference in London on 19 March. Ray Smithers, Director of the National Museums of Southern Rhodesia, flew to London as the story began to reach the international press. Pictures of heroic ranger Fothergill and his men wrestling with impala in waist-deep floods and hauling ungrateful warthog into small boats were soon appearing in newspapers and magazines and on newsreels all over the world. A leader in *The Field*, following the press conference, summed up public feeling with the headline 'Four Men Versus the Scandal at Kariba Dam'.

The Fauna Preservation Society appealed for £10,000 to buy outboards, boats, camping gear and medical supplies. The money soon came in. Volunteers at the rate of eight a month were carefully selected and recruited. By late April serious rescue work had begun on the Northern Rhodesian side of the imaginary line that ran down the centre of the lake dividing the two countries.

To the world, the Kariba rescue had become 'Operation Noah'. Even then it was not a combined operation, the two countries, although united with Nyasaland in Federation, acted independently. Sadly this has been an often recurring failure among conservationists including game departments and national parks of the same country. Only in recent years have 'rival' organisations seemed to realise that they are fighting on the same side.

The Southern Rhodesian team consisted of six rangers under Fothergill, one vet and 48 Africans operating from a 37-foot parent ship, the *Tuna*, and three small boats, powered by Mercury outboards. The Northern Rhodesian team led by Taed Edelmann, a Polish-born ranger and ex-wartime RAF pilot, was made up of two European assistants and 15 Africans equipped with one 18-foot boat and one dinghy. This small force was augmented by the Game and Hunting Association's team of 32 volunteers and three steel boats. Public opinion in Britain had now been stirred and further subscriptions provided a 45-foot parent boat powered by two Perkins diesels.

The parent ship, vital for transporting supplies and towing the smaller boats, would not be ready until October 1959, but she would still be in plenty of time for the work that lay ahead. In September the height of the water was 1,475 feet. The maximum level of 1,590 feet would not be reached until 1964. Before Operation Noah was over there would be a further 500 islands to be cleared.

I am indebted to Lieutenant-Colonel R. A. Critchley, President of the Game and Hunting Association of Northern Rhodesia, for these first-hand accounts given in *Oryx*, the journal of the Fauna Preservation Society, of what the rescue at Kariba was really like.

We went to an island in the Simamba area which was known to hold a herd of 20 to 30 impala. The island was about 300 yards long by 80 yards across, very stony and rising about 35 feet above the water at one end. The vegetation had been grazed and browsed fairly heavily but was not eaten right out. About 100 yards of game nets which we had brought with us were erected across the waist of the island and several attempts were made to drive the impala into them. These were unsuccessful as the impala refused to face the nets, one duiker ram only being caught. The nets were then moved and set up at an acute angle with the shoreline and the impala driven into the tunnel so formed. This was immediately successful, seven animals being caught. These were bound, ear-tagged, and off-loaded on to the mainland. Several more drives resulted in a total of 16 impala being netted the first day. We returned to the island the following morning, again lifted the nets and set them up in a similar position but very close to the high end of the island where the impala had sought refuge. The rest of the herd were rounded up with comparative ease, only the very last animals taking to the water. Thus the entire herd of 26 animals was removed and some valuable lessons in the siting and erection of the nets learned.

When we first landed on this island three kudu cows together with a calf between two and three months old immediately took to the water and swam 100 yards to an adjacent island. During the course of the driving another calf only two or three weeks old was found and captured. The four kudu were driven off the second island to a third, the bigger calf being captured in the water. During the night, the mother of the baby returned to the first island in search of her calf and was driven off again in the morning. From the third island the kudu were again driven off into the water and attempts were made to shepherd them in the right direction. They returned to the island

and took off again, this time in the direction of the mainland, but by the time the boat got round the island through the trees they had disappeared. They were swimming strongly and doubtless reached the mainland only a quarter of a mile away.

A steenbok doe with a lamb about two or three months old were both caught in the water and transported ashore. A klipspringer was noosed in a rocky cranny and captured.

In another part of the lake, Taed Edelmann made three attempts to rescue three cow elephants with two small calves. Thunderflashes were used to try and frighten them off, but were of no avail. The calves were caught and taken to the mainland but had to be taken back again as they could not fend for themselves and their mothers refused to leave the island. During further attempts, one cow elephant had to be shot in self-defence. The island was then left for a week. Another visit revealed that the cows had departed, leaving the two calves dead. Examination of the calves showed that they had been badly knocked about. Did their mothers kill them before they left?

In the days of Operation Noah, the business of saving and trans-locating wildlife in danger was in its infancy. Drugs for immobilisation and tranquillisation were still being developed. The vets and rangers at Kariba did their gallant best but without the store of knowledge at their disposal which rapidly built up in the next ten years. They were acting on commonsense and tried veterinary principles. Nevertheless a good deal was learned the hard way about capturing and moving wild animals. Colonel Critchley records:

When animals are captured it has been found that their temperatures rise considerably – impala are perhaps affected most of all. If released on dry land after their boat journey, they tend to lie exhausted for a few moments before slowly moving off into the bush. They are therefore put into the water a few yards from shore. This immersion brings down their body temperature and on reaching *terra firma* they shake their coats and bound off into the trees in a jaunty manner.

The treatment of an animal before it is crated varies according to its condition. A tranquillizer such as Largactyl may be necessary and intravenous injection of Sulpamethazine is used to ward off pneumonia due to shock. It is hoped that Dr A. M. Harthoorn who has done much experimental work in Uganda in the immobilization, tranquillization and movement of animals will shortly visit Kariba to give us the benefit of his advice. Particularly valuable will be his knowledge of the Palmer Cap-Chur gun and crossbow and the correct dosage to be used in the immobilizing dart which these weapons fire.*

Darting techniques, as will shortly be seen, were to play a key part in the business of saving wildlife in the immediate future. But at Kariba, unfortunately, the drugs shot into marooned rhinos had fatal results in many cases.

Kariba was a key date in conservation for many reasons. Operation Noah proved to be the great divide in the techniques of saving endangered wild animals. While the dam and its consequences showed that there were individuals who were willing to go to great lengths and to dip their hands deep into their pockets to conserve wildlife, it revealed the lack of awareness and even total disregard for the environment of which industry and governments were and are capable. It also highlighted the effects of non-co-operation between organisations and governments that are by no means unknown 40 years later.

The dam was, without doubt, an economic necessity. The shattering thing is that the planners appeared not to have considered what the lake that they created would do to the abundant fauna of the Zambesi Valley.

Since Operation Noah, industry, politicians, even governments are anxious, at least on the surface, to clean, or rather green, up their acts. The danger that they will go ahead regardless is, however, always there. What are a few seabirds and sea mammals so long as the super-tankers get the oil out? What do the caribou herds matter so long as the pipeline goes through? Are these not acceptable risks when set against the profits for the company, the dividends for the shareholders and the material gains for us all?

The list of projects potentially damaging to the ecology can be

---

* Some interesting wildlife statistics emerged from Operation Noah. The swimming capabilities of animals rescued: Leopard, waterbuck, bushbuck: one and a half miles; Kudu, one mile; zebra, 600 yards; warthog, 500 yards; baboon and aardvark, 400 yards; impala, 300 yards; vervet monkey, 200 yards; dassie (hyrax), 25 yards; squirrel: 10 yards.

Principal animals saved at Kariba by Operation Noah up to 31 July 1959: aardvark 35; bushbuck, 168; bushpig, 21; dassie, 68; duiker, 300; genets, 33; greater kudu, 112; hare, 31; impala, 469; klipspringer, 13; mongoose, 33; monkeys, 74; porcupine, 26; sable antelope, 12; steenbok, 236; warthog, 160; waterbuck, 73; zebra, 1.

extended almost indefinitely. Egypt's High Aswan Dam was a triumph of Soviet engineering. No-one foresaw that it would block the flow of life-giving silt that once fertilised the fields along the banks of the Nile downstream. Nor is it always wildlife or the environment that is put at risk. Did anyone foresee that the immense Lake Nasser which the dam created would make its own climate and introduce humidity for the first time for thousands of years into the Valley of the Kings? The monuments left to us by the ancient Egyptians are in danger of deteriorating after five thousand years of protection in hot, dry air.

Operation Noah was a turning point for two reasons. If large numbers of animals died in the waters of Lake Kariba, then their death by drowning stirred public opinion throughout the world. Kariba also provided a marker for industry and governments. They knew that henceforward their schemes would be watched more and more closely.

*

If the rescue at Kariba was crude, what came next was even more so. I know because for a short time I was part of the operation concerned. It centred on a small pocket of white rhinos in the Madi District of West Nile Province in northern Uganda. Both black and white rhinos are easy animals to poach. Their horn is the prize. Though it is merely composed of compacted hair, it commands a high price in the Far East. In India it is believed to have aphrodisiac qualities. In China and the Far East rhino horn is an ingredient in many traditional remedies, though, of course, by the standards of western medicine it is no more use than chopped hair. In 1961, the few remaining white rhinos in Uganda were in grave danger of being wiped out. It was therefore decided to capture as many as possible and move them to Murchison Falls National Park 60 miles to the south of Madi District. Though the white rhino is a very different animal from its distant black relation, there seemed no reason to believe that the drugs which had killed black rhinos at Kariba would be any safer in this operation.

The difference between the two species needs a note of explanation. It extends far beyond colour. Any rhino, any large animal for that matter, becomes the colour of the last mud in which it has wallowed. Give both black and white rhinos a good bath in the nearest river and they emerge an identical shade of battleship grey. There the similarities between the two species end, given the fact that they are both quite evidently rhinos and carry two large horns on the ends of their noses. In looks, the white rhino is altogether bulkier, its head longer, its snout blunt. Whereas the black rhino's snout is tucked in at the lips, making it thoroughly mean-looking, the white rhino has a wideness of mouth that gives a clue as to how it got its name. The belief is that the early Dutch settlers in South Africa described it as having a *weide monde*, a wide mouth, and in time the word *weide* became white. By some strange zoological circumstance there is a large gap in the white rhino population that stretched from northern Uganda, Zaire, and the Sudan to South Africa, notably Natal, with not a white rhino in between.

Because of the bad experience at Kariba, no-one was willing to take the risk of using immobilising drugs on the few surviving Ugandan rhino. The decision was taken by the Game Department, in whose territory the remaining rhino lived, together with the Uganda Parks authorities into whose safe-keeping they were to be transferred, to capture the animals by old-fashioned game-catching methods, namely by lassoing them. There were in Kenya several experts in this somewhat perilous field, perhaps the most famous of whom was Carr Hartley. Uganda chose a man called Ken Randall who, with his team, wanted some young hippos that were then fetching a good price in zoos. The Uganda Parks, as we have seen, had a surplus of hippos, and Randall and his partner, Pat O'Connell, were to be allowed to catch several young hippo around the Kazinga Channel in the Queen Elizabeth National Park. In exchange they would move 400 miles north to Madi District to catch as many white rhinos as possible before the poachers got them, or the rains came and made further catching impossible. After a settling down period in bomas, or holding pens, the white rhinos would be moved by road to Murchison Falls National Park and, after another acclimatisation period, released. There it was hoped they would breed in the wild and re-establish a Ugandan dynasty of a dying species, the northern race of the white rhino. It was in every sense a classic example of saving them.

My part in what became known as 'SOS Rhino' was to join the catchers and make a film about the whole crazy wild west exercise. I took with me John Buxton, a British wildlife cameraman more used to filming marsh harriers in Norfolk than rhino in Africa. We were both, in fact, as green as elephant grass after the rains.

In Uganda we co-opted the aid of a character almost as bizarre as the catchers themselves. Chiels Margach, a Scot and one of the few white settlers in Uganda, was a trustee of the Uganda Parks. Chiels – I believe the name derived from the Scottish diminutive for 'child' – was a keen amateur naturalist who owned a pineapple, pawpaw and ginger plantation at Masindi, 50 miles south of Murchison. He also owned a clockwork-driven Bolex 16mm movie camera, an iron nerve, and a venerable Stinson Reliant highwing monoplane which he flew from a grass strip among his pawpaw trees. When in the air he invariably wore a planter's straw hat almost as wide as the cockpit. Chiels' utter calm reassured two inexperienced film-makers when all about were losing theirs. He was a great comfort and not a bad second cameraman.

Lassoing white rhino is an occupation that takes a little getting used to. Previously only two white rhinos, young ones, had even been caught by this method. Coincidentally, this feat had been performed by another Norfolkman, Edward Seago. No-one, including the catchers, knew how a fully grown white rhino would behave when forcibly attached to a lasso. The general opinion was that it would fail to live up to its reputation for peaceful co-existence with people. For once, general opinion was right.

The technique was simple, even crude. The catching truck was an ancient ex-WD Ford 15 Cwt. Bolted to its sides were six tree trunks. These acted as bollards to which a one-inch sisal lasso rope could be fastened once it was attached to the rhino. The nooses of the lassos were fixed to the end of 10-foot bamboo poles with wire and insulating tape that would break once any strain was put on it by a well-hooked rhino.

For the first catch I was given the passenger's seat alongside Ken Randall who captained the team and drove. The team behind the cab in the open back of the truck consisted of Pat O'Connell, Ken Stewart and Louie Wedd, Ken's son-in-law, together with various Luo, Turkana and Kikuyu handlers. They were all veterans and plainly regarded John Buxton, Margach and myself as an unnecessary evil whose only justification was that Anglia Television (of whose 'Survival' natural history unit I was the head) was to some extent under-writing the operation. If we fell off the truck during a catch, then no-one would stop to pick us up. If we got in the way of the roping operation, we were quite likely to be pushed overboard anyway. If we rode with them, they made quite clear, we did so at our own risk. Nothing must get in the way of catching the rhinos and that included us. Once these rather gritty introductions had been made we all got on extremely well.

The noise of the catching truck screaming along in third gear as it demolished trees and tore through 10-foot-high elephant grass is something I shall not easily, if ever, forget. There was quite a lot of tall grass, and once we had plunged into it, it was like being under water. The driver could see nothing. Navigation was controlled by a hand that appeared through the hatch in the roof of the cab and signalled in which direction to steer. The remote control helmsman above the cab could see over the grass. What he could not see was down into it. Termite mounds and hyena holes abounded. We hit these with back-shattering frequency. When we emerged from the grass, however, the first target was in sight. It was a very large target. In fact, it turned out to be the largest land animal ever persuaded into captivity, a 3½-ton white rhino cow with calf at foot. When finally we caught up with them, Randall gently edged the cow away with what remained of his offside front wing. O'Connell dropped the rope over the calf's tiny horn. The big cow swerved away and then put in a couple of false charges in an attempt to rescue her child. John Heppes of the Game Department who had accompanied us in his Land Rover – it was his game scouts who had found the rhinos for us in the first place – put in a false charge of his own. Possibly the big cow thought she was being attacked by the catching trucks' own calf. She finally backed off and watched us warily from under a tree some 200 yards away. Randall explained that if he had gone for the mother first, the baby might have wandered off into the scrub, got lost and become a victim of a lion. The calf gave little trouble, was soon roped and transferred to the 3-ton truck that was following us up.

'Mum', said O'Connell, 'is going to be something different.' She was.

The cow took off at a gallop into the elephant grass as soon as she heard the truck coming. When we finally roared alongside her, she hooked savagely at the bonnet with her three-foot-long front horn. The horn was longer than anything the catchers had met with to date. When the time came to rope, O'Connell could not get the noose over the tip of the horn and down over her snout. John Buxton, who was gallantly filming this up top while clinging on for his life, afterwards told me what had happened. Louie Wedd apparently crossed to O'Connell's side, managed to lengthen his own noose and drop it over the cow's huge horn; I quote from the account I wrote soon afterwards:

Randall drove the 15–Cwt round her in a slow circle, keeping her on a tight line while the animal fought it out. Without warning, the rhino changed tactics. She galloped left-handed across our front so that the rope whipped over our screen and strained out at a 45 degree angle on the nearside of the truck. Now the rhino was looking at me and I began to feel very acutely the absence of a door on my side of the cab. The fact that Randall had assured me a door was no protection if a rhino really decided to come aboard was little comfort. The rhino almost seemed to guess what I was feeling for she came straight in and charged. At first her trajectory seemed to be taking her right into the cab. I wriggled off my seat and shared the centre of the floor with the gear lever. But at the last second she swerved and the uppercut she gave with her horn hit the body low down just forward of the cab. The tip of her horn appeared through the metal.

There was something utterly primeval about this furious animal seen at close quarters and I do not mind admitting that I have seldom been so frightened.

She didn't back away but stayed where she was, lunging and lunging with her horn and rocking the truck with every slash. I had had enough. Ken Stewart had told me the night before that if a rhino really did stick its head into the cab there was always an escape route through the hatch in the cab roof. I used it now and emerged on top of the cab just as the animal made a run round the front. I felt the rope moving under me and jumped just in time to save myself from being swept to the ground. The rhino had by no means finished yet. She was giving the treatment to the front of the bonnet now, alternating uppercuts with trip-hammer blows on top of the radiator by letting her head crash down on it. You had the feeling of being on a very small tin island being battered by monstrous seas.

What O'Connell did at this monent fills me with admiration even to this day. He went over the side with a short length of rope in his hands, and, while the rhino was busy savaging the front of the truck, nipped practically under her belly and got a rope round one back leg. This, it seemed, was the moment of truth in rhino-catching. Once the back legs were haltered, a good deal of the steam went out of the creature. Wedd was still in the truck shortening rope round one of the tree trunk bollards. The rest of the Lilliputians now swarmed over the cow. O'Connell, Randall and the African ropers slipped and tightened a second rope round her front legs and then all heaved together so that she went down on her side. As O'Connell had predicted: it had been 'a big one'.

The huge beast had then to be loaded. A pit was dug in the bush close to the trussed and now fairly docile animal and the 3-ton truck was then backed down into it. The tailboard was lowered and metal rollers placed between tailboard and the rhino's stern. Everything including the animal was now drenched with water. A wire cable was attached by a hook to the rope tied round the captive's rear legs. The wire ran round a pulley in the back of the 3-tonner and thence to the catching truck. At a signal from Randall, Wedd drove the truck slowly forward. The rhino was thus dragged a few feet at a time up the ramp and into the lorry. It was not a pretty sight. Every now and again, she raised her head in protest and brought it down with a crash onto the metal rollers. Randall winced each time as though it was his own head that was taking the punishment. He really cared about his rhinos.

The big cow and the calf survived their ordeal. All told, 10 white rhino were caught and moved by road to Murchison Falls; four of these died. Those that remained in the wild in Madi District did not escape the poachers for very long. The six survivors that Ken Randall caught settled down in Murchison and started to breed. SOS Rhino has to be rated a success by the standards that existed at the time. It was a turning point in the drive to save large animals. It was the last time that such crude and potentially damaging methods were to be used. Six more white rhinos were captured by darting in 1964 and added to the Murchison stock. Alas, the Murchison Falls white rhinos were not to enjoy the sanctuary of the park for very long.

★

The northern race of the white rhino is now extinct in Uganda. In 1948 the population had been estimated at 190 animals. Many of these had lived along the Nile in the Ajai-Inde swamps and 40 miles to the north of Obongi in the Mount Kei Reserve, as well as in the neighbouring Otze Forest Sanctuary. There were thought to have been another 75 along the Uganda-Sudan border. Thanks to improved anti-poaching operations by the Game Department, numbers built up. In the first half of the 1950s some authorities put the total population as high as 500 and certainly no lower than 300. The rot started in 1956 with heavily increased poaching from over the border in the Sudan. Numbers fell everywhere, so much so that the Game Department started to consider translocating as many as possible to Murchison Falls National Park. The 1961 operation described above was the first attempt. Six more rhinos were darted and moved into the park in 1964. The 12 animals there began breeding and were thought to be sufficient to ensure the survival of the white rhino in Uganda. By 1974 there were at least 30 in Murchison. Outside the park in the Ajai-Inde reserve and along the Sudanese border poachers were fast wiping out the few rhinos left. Murchison Falls, now re-christened Kabalega National Park, was the only hope. Sadly, the regime responsible for changing the park's name put an end to that hope. During the dreadful days of Idi Amin, and the civil wars that followed, most of the elephants and all the white rhino in the park were wiped out by the rival forces and by poachers who found it easy to obtain automatic weapons from any faction that cared to sell their arms. The days of the northern race of the white rhino in Uganda were over.

5

Put your Pennies in the Panda

Everything that had happened during the 1950s showed the need for dedicated and expert people if we were to save endangered wild animals. It had become equally clear, and was forcibly demonstrated throughout Operation Noah at Kariba that, no matter how dedicated the rangers and wardens might be, they were helpless without adequate financial backing. Of course funds have always and probably always will be in short supply for conservation. Besides this, the countries in which wildlife is most in peril are usually those that have the least money to spend on saving it. Indeed they probably have the most to gain (in the short term anyway) by wastefully exploiting it or its habitat. The fact that these countries often contain large wilderness areas, complete with a diminishing stock of wild animals, is usually an indication that they are 'developing' nations with priorities other than saving wildlife. So-called 'developed' nations tend to have long since obliterated wilderness and their wild populations in the name of progress!

In 1961, something took place to change the picture radically. It all started with a letter written by Victor Stolan, a wealthy naturalised Briton from Central Europe, who had read three articles written for the *Observer* by Sir Julian Huxley, after a visit to East Africa. Sir Julian, perhaps the most distinguished biologist of his day, warned that unless something was done soon, the wildlife riches of East Africa would disappear within the next twenty years. Stolan, who had not hitherto been a wildlife enthusiast, was so moved by these articles that he wrote:

A single and uninhibited mind must take charge of such a world-embracing situation. I hasten to add that I am not such a person. However, I have some ideas as to how to collect substantial donations but have nobody of sufficient importance to speak to. Would

40

you care to put me in touch with somebody with whom such ideas can
be developed and speedily directed towards accumulating some
millions of pounds without mobilising commissions and committees
etc. as there is no time for Victorian procedure?

Stolan was perhaps a little over-optimistic in this last plea, but not in
his final sentence. 'There must be a way', he continued, 'to the
conscience and heart and pride and vanity of the very rich people to
persuade them to sink their hands deeply into their pockets.'

Huxley passed the letter to the then Director of the Nature Conservancy Council, Max Nicholson, a man of great drive and imagination
who has been too little honoured for the part he has played in
conservation. Nicholson in turn contacted Peter Scott who had already
established the Wildfowl Trust in 1946 and who certainly had some
experience of appealing to the rich. Scott, Nicholson and Guy Mountfort, a keen ornithologist and, more important, the Managing Director
of the large advertising agency Mather and Crowther, had already
talked about creating a fund-raising organisation at a private dinner
several months previously. Mountfort was in many ways exactly the
sort of man Stolan had had in mind. Top advertising executives not
only have promotional ideas but industrial contacts, and ways of
selling their ideas to such contacts. With the new impetus from Stolan,
Mountfort was approached at a meeting of the British Ornithologists'
Union in York, and it was due to his enthusiasm that a blueprint for an
international fund-raising organisation was drawn up. There would be
Swiss, German, Dutch and Austrian Appeals with other nations to
follow. Prince Philip agreed to become President of the British Appeal
and Prince Bernhard of the Netherlands was invited to become
International President.

The obvious place for an international headquarters was at Morges
in Switzerland, partly because of its banking facilities but also because
the International Union for the Conservation of Nature (IUCN), with
which Sir Julian Huxley was closely connected already, had its offices
there. The new organisation set up in the same building. Indeed it had
at first been proposed that it should be part of IUCN but wiser
counsels prevailed, suggesting that science and fund-raising would be
better kept in separate compartments. So, under Swiss law, the World
Wildlife Fund was born, with the subtitle, An International Charitable
Foundation for Saving the World's Wildlife and Wild Places.

The target was to collect £2 million annually for the first few years;
sights would be raised after that. Max Nicholson's blueprint laid down
that one third of each donation would be deposited in the central

account in Switzerland, one third would go to the national appeal concerned and the remaining third would go to whatever project most needed it at that time. The short term objective was to give grants to save animals that were immediately threatened. The long term object-ive was environmental education in the broadest sense.

The World Wildlife Fund (renamed The World Wide Fund for Nature in 1988) got off to a flying start. In Britain, where it all began, this was largely due to the imagination of its first honorary Public Relations Chief, Ian McPhail, who later became the International Campaigns Director. Like Guy Mountfort, McPhail was in advertising and public relations and he persuaded Hugh Cudlipp, editor of the *Daily Mirror*, to publish a shock issue to mark the launching of the World Wildlife Fund, known thereafter as WWF. Max Nicholson was dead against the idea, declaring in heated debate with MacPhail that the *Mirror* would not convey the right image for an organisation headed by Prince Philip. MacPhail thought that the Prince would be the first to understand the popular appeal and pulling power of the *Mirror*. He wanted Nicholson to stick to the scientific and planning side of things, at which he was unrivalled, while he was left alone to get on with what he best understood, public relations. MacPhail won the argument.

The WWF was launched in September, 1961, at a meeting at the Royal Society of Arts in London. On 8 October, at Cudlipp's invita-tion, MacPhail was 'on the stone' as the *Mirror* was put to bed, helping to design seven pages of their shock issue. The front page carried an enormous headline 'DOOMED', beneath which ran the subhead 'To disappear from the face of the earth due to Man's Greed and Neglect'. Below this appeared an almost full-page picture of Gertie and her calf. Gertie was the famous rhino of Amboseli in Kenya who carried a freak horn over 4 feet long and who, predictably was slain by poachers some years later. The *Mirror* issue may not have been precisely what Victor Stolan had had in mind when he talked of persuading the very rich to dig deep into their pockets but it was, as Max Nicholson later acknow-ledged, enormously successful. The shock edition raised £60,000 from *Mirror* readers, the equivalent in 1990 terms of close to £250,000.

In one area there was, surprisingly, a major disappointment. The American Appeal, under the auspices of President Eisenhower, failed to generate much enthusiasm. The reasons were not hard to find. Americans felt they were a long way from the threatened elephants and rhinos of Africa. They had their own long-established federal and state wildlife organisations, not to mention well-run national parks and refuges. Perhaps more important was the powerful presence of existing

conservation bodies such as the National Audubon Society and, for the
rich, the Sierra Club. It took some time to break down this isolationist
attitude. Encouragement came from such blandishments as the Thousand and One Club, which asked for 1,000 well-heeled people each to
subscribe $10,000 to the WWF. In return for this they would receive
VIP treatment if they chose to go on safari to Serengeti. Few actually
did so, but the honour of belonging to this exclusive club flattered the
necessary 1,000 members, not all of whom were Americans. Victor
Stolan, who died within a few years of WWF's foundation, would
certainly have approved.

In its first year WWF funded 20 projects – including, with help from
the Fauna Preservation Society of London, the capture of the last
Arabian Oryx. These were transferred to safety in Phoenix, Arizona,
until numbers could be built up sufficiently for them to be returned to
the Arabian desert. It also arranged the purchase of one of the most
important wetlands in southern Europe, the Marismas, the marshes
bordering the River Guadalquivir in southern Spain, which were vital
to the migration of waterbirds to and from Africa. The Ugandan white
rhino catch (previously described) and, dear to Peter Scott's heart, the
return to their native islands of 30 ne-ne, or Hawaiian geese, were also
achieved. Between its foundation and 1989 WWF has supported more
than 5,000 conservation projects worldwide and spent over £81 million
on these operations and purchases. In a typical year in the United
Kingdom alone, grants for around 160 projects are approved and a sum
of around £700,000 spent on them.

Inevitably, the World Wide Fund for Nature, (to give it its new
title*) has not escaped criticism. It has been accused of failing to save
the elephant and rhino, though it is hard to see how it could have done
so, and of wasting £1 million in China on fruitlessly trying to save the
giant panda. Yet, all in all, WWF has succeeded beyond the dreams of
Victor Stolan and probably even beyond those of the late Sir Peter
Scott to whose gifts, energy and talents conservation owes more than to
almost any other single man. WWF pledged itself to educate in the
broadest sense and this has been its greatest achievement. It has played
a significant part in persuading many industries and some governments

---

* It can be taken as a sign of general environmental awareness that three of
the most influential conservation bodies, two British and one international,
have changed their titles to include habitat as well as animals; the Fauna
Preservation Society to the Fauna and Flora Preservation Society, the
Wildfowl Trust to the Wildfowl and Wetland Trust, and the World
Wildlife Fund to the World Wide Fund for Nature.

that it is good for their image, at the very least, to appear conservation-minded. It has also played a large part in 'greening' the outlook of the average person. The cuddly panda logo, often fashioned as a collecting box, has brought in more than millions of pennies; it has engendered sympathy. The success of the panda appeal perfectly illustrates how environmental awareness can be created by focusing attention on saving attractive wildlife. Practically everything else, from the need for cleaner bathing beaches to the demand for organically grown food, follows from that.

In 1961, at about the time when the WWF was being prepared for its launch, another key event took place. The setting for it was the small town of Arusha in Tanzania, some 150 miles from what is still the greatest wildlife spectacle on earth, the plains of Serengeti with their millions of migrating animals. The three new East African nations of Uganda, Kenya and Tanzania had either gained their independence from British colonial rule, or were about to do so.

When, in 1946, King George VI opened the first East African National Park on the outskirts of Nairobi, he declared: 'The wildlife of today is not ours to dispose of as we please. We have it in trust. We must account for it to those who come after.' This praiseworthy sentiment was inscribed above the main gate of Nairobi Park and remains there to this day. The King, or his speech-writer, had come up with a pledge that stood a good chance of being honoured so long as the British were in power. But suddenly, in 1961, *uhuru* (freedom) was won and independence granted. Would the three emergent African nations, with all their economic and social problems, feel the same about wildlife? It seemed extremely doubtful. Could they be persuaded to protect their unique wildlife heritage? Could they be given good reasons for doing so, reasons which would appeal to their enlightened self-interest? It was to put across such ideas that the Arusha Conference was arranged.

The Conference was, in fact, Stage Two of the Special African Project of the IUCN, and so the international conservationists already involved in the embryonic World Wildlife Fund played a leading part at Arusha too. Careful preparation had led to thinking that was a long way from WWF's cuddly panda approach. The fact that most Africans, whether politicians or small farmers, did not feel the same way about wildlife as did Westerners had to be faced. New African politicians were likely to be tempted to put land that had been successfully used by wildlife for thousands of years to purposes for which it was unsuited – either growing crops or grazing cattle. The African with a *shamba*, or small-holding, could not be expected to admire elephants or buffalo. They were not only dangerous but they trampled his meagre crops. Means had to be found of persuading African rulers that it was to their advantage to keep national parks and reserves going and, if possible, to set up new ones.

The Conference met under the patronage of Julius Nyerere, then Prime Minister of the new Tanzania, formerly Tanganyika, and later to become its President. Privately, the scholarly and liberally-minded Prime Minister admitted that looking at wild animals was not to his personal taste, though he recognised that others found great joy and satisfaction in the pursuit. Whatever he may have said off the record, his conference declaration left no doubt where he stood politically. His statement was written by Ian MacPhail; it was no politician's hand-out. MacPhail recalls that Nyerere dissected every sentence and contested small points of meaning until he was quite satisfied. The Arusha Declaration has since become a conservation classic.

The survival of our wildlife is a matter of great concern to all of us in Africa. These wild creatures and the wild places they inhabit are not only important as a source of wonder and inspiration but are an integral part of our future livelihood and well-being. In accepting the trusteeship of our wildlife we solemnly declare that we will do everything in our power to make sure that our children's grand-children will be able to enjoy this rich and precious inheritance.

The conservation of wildlife and wild places calls for specialist knowledge, trained manpower and money and we look to other nations to co-operate in this important task, the success or failure of which not only affects the Continent of Africa but the rest of the world as well.

It was a statesmanlike document which made clear what the Prime Minister wanted in return. His government later kept its word faith-fully, as did the government of Kenya. (Uganda would probably have done just as well had not the black anarchy of Amin's rule obliterated the majority of its more spectacular animals.) The international con-servationists at Arusha appreciated that solid reasons for saving wild animal populations must be presented to the new African leaders. Among the reasons put to them were:

1 Well maintained national parks would attract increasing numbers of tourists and bring in a great deal of hard currency.

This prediction could hardly have been more accurate. Wildlife-oriented tourism was to become one of the most important, possibly *the* most important source of revenue for some states, Kenya in particular.

2 The rest of the world would look up to and respect emergent nations who were prepared to protect their wild heritage.

3 Help in the form of funds and scientists would, as Nyerere had requested, be forthcoming. The most important thing, however, was to train African wardens and biologists to do the job themselves.

Before many years had passed, an African wildlife college, partly funded by the WWF, was opened at Mweka in Tanzania with just this purpose.

4 Wild animals usually make far better use of land than domestic stock. Game ranching for meat had been tried successfully in South Africa and might well prove beneficial in East African countries.

This proposition did not run contrary to conservation ideas. A surplus of, say, Thomson's gazelle can be cropped only if there is a sufficient basic stock from which to take it.

Not everything has worked out. The appalling and accelerating slaughter of elephants and rhinos has horrified not only the African countries but the rest of the world. Nevertheless, looking back over thirty years, there is no doubt that the spirit of the Arusha Conference has lasted surprisingly well.

*

Among the wildlife experts at Arusha was a German with an almost unpronounceable name – Bernhard Grzimek (the 'rz' is silent and the 'G' becomes a 'J') who had special affiliations with Tanzania. These went beyond a sentimental attachment to a former German colony. In 1961 Grzimek's name was synonymous with the Serengeti. With his son Michael, he made an Oscar-winning film called *Serengeti Shall Not Die*, and followed it with a book of the same title. Indeed, the Grzimeks were not only fund-raisers, propagandists, authors and film-makers, they were scientists too. The results they achieved were the more remarkable because they did not have a large organisation to back them. Outside Germany, where Bernhard appeared regularly in his own television show, the name Grzimek is virtually unknown, yet he did more in the cause of saving wild animals than any other individual simply because he did it single-handed. Professor of Giessen University, Bernhard Grzimek was also Director of Frankfurt Zoo, one of the most successful and imaginative zoos in Europe if not the world. A handsome, rather Prussian-officer-looking man, Grzimek was certainly no militarist and can have had little sympathy with Nazi Germany. During the Second World War he served in the German Army as a vet. Grzimek summed up his philosophy thus:

Millions feared Hitler and millions were enthralled by him. Millions laid down their lives for him and other millions died fighting against him. Today when German school children are asked questions about Hitler most of them know very little about him and cannot even name his henchmen. Men are easily inspired by human ideas but they forget them just as quickly. Only nature is eternal, unless we senselessly destroy it. In 50 years' time nobody will be interested in the results of conferences which fill today's headlines. But when, 50 years from now, a lion walks into the red dawn and roars resoundingly, it will mean something to people and quicken their hearts whether they are bolsheviks or democrats, or whether they speak English, German, Russian or Swahili. They will stand in quiet awe as, for the first time in their lives, they watch 20,000 zebras wander across the endless plains. Is it really so stupid to work for zebras, lions and men who will walk the earth 50 years from now? And for those in 100 or 200 years' time?

Bernhard Grzimek's fight for the future security of the Serengeti deserves a special place in the history of conservation. It was a battle he shared with his son Michael for whom it was to end in death. As a boy, Michael helped his father in behaviourist studies with dogs and wolves. He took up animal photography with a stills camera and later with a movie camera. In the late 1950s his father wrote a bestseller, *No Room for Wild Animals*, about the plight of African wildlife. Michael made a documentary film based on this book against all the odds and cries of doom from distributors – their chief complaint was that the animals were shown as being too peaceable. There was not enough blood and danger, and what American television bosses refer to as 'jeopardy'. Despite these handicaps the film not only scooped the major prizes at the 1957 Berlin Film Festival but ran for 12 weeks in one of Munich's biggest cinemas. Later it was shown in 63 countries.

The film attacked the British government's proposal to lop one third off the area of the Serengeti National Park; the Grzimeks pledged one third of the film's revenue to buying land to *add* to the threatened

Serengeti plains. When Peter Molloy, Director of the National Parks of Tanganyika, heard of this, he flew to Frankfurt and made the Grzimeks a counter-proposal. The intended excision of one third of the park's land was based on unproven assumptions about how the Serengeti's million animals, and in particular the vast wildebeest herds, moved on annual migration. Any plan to cut off one third of the park and give it over to tribal grazing was therefore founded on guesswork. If the true facts could be discovered, then the government might be persuaded to relent. The Grzimeks were excited by the idea but how could this work be carried out over such a vast area, parts of which were often impassable in the rainy season, even to four-wheel drive vehicles? There was only one answer: learn to fly, buy a suitable aeroplane and then take it out to Tanganyika to conduct aerial surveys, as well as make ground counts and movement studies.

Michael was a natural pilot. His father flew because a co-pilot was necessary and because he felt he had to keep an eye on his son. The aircraft they bought was a vastly improved and more powerful version of the Fieseler *Storch* (Stork), the highly adaptable light aircraft which the Luftwaffe and German Army had used for spotting and communications in the Second World War. The great virtue of the *Storch* was that it could land in a very small space. Throttled back, and on full flap, the aircraft could stay in the air at only 30 mph. Its American Lycoming engine gave it a top speed of 140 mph. Partly as a publicity gimmick, but also because they wanted their aircraft to be visible in the event of a forced landing far out in the bush, they had it painted in zebra stripes. The relative values of visibility and publicity must be judged from the fact that the zebra has spent millions of years evolving its striped camouflage in order to become invisible in a shimmering heat haze. No matter, the zebra-striped *Storch* was in keeping with the spirit of daring and adventure that surrounded what was, at heart, a serious scientific expedition.

On 11 December 1957, father and son set off on what was to be their first big cross-country flight – from Germany to Tanganyika. In the next two years, the Grzimeks flew thousands of hours over the plains of Serengeti, an area twice the size of Devonshire. They drove thousands of miles in their zebra-striped Land Rover. Together with the pioneer wardens of the Serengeti, notably Myles Turner and Gordon Poolman, they invented ways of catching and marking zebra and wildebeest so that the migrations of the great herds could be studied and understood for the first time.

Previously, the experts advising the British government had argued that the north-western part of the Serengeti was not used by the herds;

that the mass of wildebeest found in the centre of the plains during the height of the migration came from two sources, the thin corridor of park stretching towards Lake Victoria to the west and the beautiful Ngorongoro Crater, at that time inside park boundaries, on the eastern side. This view had been put forward to the colonial government in the Pearsall Report two years before the Grzimeks flew their *Storch* from Germany. On the strength of it the government proposed to carve up the Serengeti. To the east, Ngorongoro, the great caldera (or collapsed volcano), large enough to hold the city of Paris and its suburbs, would be taken away from the park, as would Olduvai Gorge, where Louis and Mary Leakey made their historic fossil finds of early man.

At the end of their two-year study, Bernhard and Michael Grzimek had established beyond doubt that the premises on which the Pearsall Report was founded were unsound. For example, the wildebeest herds never, as had been assumed for years, moved out of the Ngorongoro Crater to join those from the western corridor on the central plains. They stayed inside the crater all the year round. Their findings were spectacularly recorded in the Grzimeks' film, *Serengeti Shall Not Die*, which won a 'best documentary' Oscar, and Bernhard's bestseller of the same name.

Tragedy marked the end of their venture. One afternoon Michael took off in their plane on a routine filming reconnaissance. It was to be a long trip over Lengai, the active volcano that is the sacred mountain of the Maasai, and on over the Gol Mountains and the great soda lake Natron, where most of the Rift Valley flamingoes nest. Bernhard had asked his son not to leave his return too late. It made him nervous waiting for the sound of the engine as the shadows lengthened and darkness fell, as it does in the tropics with the sudden finality of a falling curtain. Michael agreed. He would land at a park post, Banagi, and fly on the next morning. Somewhere over the plateau at the top of the Gols, in whose cliffs nest the Griffon vultures, one of these great birds struck the right wing and bent it backwards, jamming the control cables. The *Storch* dived from 600 feet, killing Michael instantly. He was buried the next day on the green rim looking down into the Ngorongoro Crater. I have stood by the stone and read its inscription.

MICHAEL GRZIMEK
12.4.1934 – 10.1.1959
He gave all he possessed for the wild animals of Africa.

Shortly after Michael Grzimek's death and before the results of the Grzimeks' survey could be published, the British colonial government acted, as Bernhard and Michael had feared, to truncate the park. The Ngorongoro Crater, sometimes called 'the eighth wonder of the world', was turned into a conservation area where the rights of humans, notably Maasai herdsmen, took precedence, though wildlife was to remain protected. The immediate outcome was an epidemic of rhino spearing by Maasai *moran*, the young warriors who formerly proved their manhood by killing a lion. This, however, was soon brought under control with, it must be said, full co-operation from Maasai elders. Maasai and game continued to live in harmony as they had done since these pastoral nomads first moved into Tanganyika from the north. (It is sometimes forgotten that this warrior tribe is a comparative newcomer to the lands they now claim.)

All the same, the Grzimeks' work was by no means in vain. New land, admittedly of less ecological value, was added to the park on its north and south-west boundaries through the publicity given to Serengeti's needs. President Nyerere of Tanzania took a personal interest in the park, ordering human settlements on the northern and north-western borders to be moved so that the annual wildebeest migration should not be interfered with. At the same time John Owen, a tough-minded and imaginative former district commissioner, took over as Director of the Tanzanian parks. Owen saw that though the work of the Grzimeks had been immensely valuable, it had only scratched the surface where research was concerned. A Michael Grzimek Laboratory was built, largely with money raised by the book and film, and this nucleus at Seronera, the park H.Q., grew into the Serengeti Research Institute. Owen attracted many of the best young scientists to help unravel the complicated ecological mysteries of the plains. He rightly saw that, large as it was, the Serengeti could survive future pressures only if its needs were more fully understood. George Schaller (lion study), Hans Kruuk (hyenas), Murray Watson and Lee Talbot (game census) made the Serengeti a scientific Mecca for brilliant young research workers from all over the world.

Another by-product of the Grzimeks' experience was that Owen saw, probably more clearly than anyone else working in African parks at the time, the vital part that light aircraft could play in park management. Though no longer young and not possessed of the keenest eyesight he learned to fly himself and urged his senior park officers to do the same. As was the case on many other occasions it was Bernhard Grzimek and the Frankfurt Zoological Society who raised much of the money to buy Super Cubs and other small aircraft.

Three years after the Grzimeks' aerial survey ended, another census was carried out by the Royal Air Force together with a team led by Lee

The *Daily Mirror* front page that put the World Wildlife Fund on the map in 1961.

In 1957 the British government planned to reduce the area of the Serengeti National Park. Bernhard and Michael Grzimek conducted a survey from their own aircraft to prove that this territory is vital to half a million migrating animals.

Lions became frequent companions of the Grzimeks while shooting their film, *Serengeti Shall Not Die* – a powerful propaganda weapon for African wildlife.

This tranquillised lion wears an eye-shade to protect his eyes from harsh sunlight.

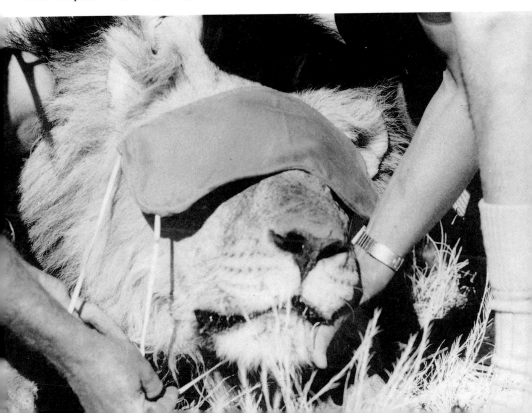

Jan Oelofse perfected a method of capturing whole herds of plains animals by driving them into an enclosure between long walls of plastic sheeting.

To appease irate farmers, Shirley Strum had to move the Pumphouse Gang of baboons (which she had been studying for more than 20 years) 80 miles up the Rift Valley.

Talbot. This survey covered a larger area and showed a considerable increase in the number of wildebeest estimated by the Grzimeks. Murray Watson made a census again in 1963 and reported a 40 per cent increase in the herds. In 1965, a further aerial count made the total 1,300,000 head of plains game. At first it was feared that this huge increase (the Grzimeks' estimate of the total was only 366,000 animals) would out-strip the grazing. Subsequent work, though, showed that the Serengeti herds are subject to large population swings dependent, among other factors, on the quality of grazing.

Serengeti still has the whole-hearted support of the Tanzanian government. Following the Arusha Conference, the government showed the value it placed on wildlife by creating four new parks at Lake Manyara, Ngurdoto Crater, Ruaha and Mikumi. Far from dying, the Serengeti itself has continued to thrive though it has, like everywhere else, suffered cruelly from heavy poaching of large animals, notably black rhino and elephant. As always, funds, or rather the shortage of them, are at the root of the problem. Tanzania has had a tough economic history. More than ever it needs the outside help that its President asked for at Arusha in 1961, as does every other country whose elephants and rhino are being decimated.

★

Soon after Michael Grzimek's death, Bernhard began fighting a new campaign, this time in support of an African national park whose existence was threatened by the civil war in the former Belgian colony, the Congo. His Serengeti experiences had shown Grzimek the value of films and television as propaganda media for conservation. To replace Michael as a wildlife cameraman he took on a young Briton, later to become a Kenyan, called Alan Root. Alan, who emerged ten years later as possibly the best wildlife film-maker in the world, became almost a surrogate son. Bernhard proposed that they make a dangerous safari across Uganda's southern border with the Congo to find out what was happening to the ranger force of the Parc Albert. Grzimek had heard that, though the European wardens had left, the African game rangers were keeping up their anti-poaching patrols and would continue so long as they were paid. Ugandan rangers from the Queen Elizabeth National Park who had crossed the border several weeks before had found abandoned houses, overturned cars, empty hospitals and dead or dying domestic stock everywhere. It seemed likely that Lumumba's guerilla troops from Stanleyville would arrive in the Parc Albert at any moment. Life, human or animal, would not be safe if they did.

Grzimek and Root reached the Parc Albert headquarters without incident, apart from being held up and having to drive for their lives at a border post, expecting a burst of automatic fire to follow them at any moment. They found that the rangers, still smart in their khaki uniforms and green fezzes, had maintained everything just as if no civil war were taking place. There had been scares. Some Lumumba troops had passed through recently, ordering the rangers to shoot any European that showed his face. Nevertheless, the African park staff served Bernhard and Alan a modest three-course meal in the restaurant. There were clean towels and sheets in the visitors' huts just as if Europeans had been calling in daily.

During their stay, Dr Jacques Verschuren, the 30-year-old Scientific Director of the park, turned up. At the time he was the foremost protagonist of the leave-nature-to-solve-her-own-problems school of thought, yet he wasn't prepared to see his rangers left to solve theirs. He alone had stayed on when the park's other European officials had left. He had been threatened with death several times by Lumumba's men. Loaded rifles had been waved in his face, and whenever the situation got too hot he had disappeared into the bush. Rebel soldiers were not too keen on places where elephants and lions roamed. Verschuren told Grzimek that it was vital to get pay for the loyal rangers. Without wages, it was highly likely that they would start killing their animal charges in order to live.

When Grzimek returned to Germany, he cabled and phoned government ministries in several countries, including Britain and the United States. No-one was willing to give money to a park in a district ruled by an illegal breakaway regime that did not even recognise the central government in Leopoldville. Not to be beaten, Grzimek raised the money through the Frankfurt Zoological Society, and purchased Congolese francs at a favourable rate of exchange. Verschuren who, to Grzimek's joy and surprise, had so far survived the civil war, flew to Frankfurt to collect the money and take it personally to the rangers at Parc Albert.*

It was the first of many such fund-raising operations that Grzimek performed. In Germany he had two powerful weapons – his own wildlife magazine called *Das Tier* and a television series. With these he

---

* In 1962 my wife and I crossed Lake Edward to the Congo side with Frank Poppleton, head warden of the Uganda parks. We found the rangers faithfully on duty at the mouth of the Semliki River. Their uniforms were as smart as ever. They were still receiving pay through the Frankfurt Zoological Society. We heard that not long after all these men were murdered by rebel troops.

did remarkable and sometimes outrageous things. Once he announced on his television programme that Lufthansa was running special excursion flights so that people could visit the African game parks. Hundreds of applicants phoned the airline – Germans are very wildlife-oriented. The airline protested that it had no such cheap flights in its schedule. 'Well,' Grzimek told them, 'now that you've got all these bookings you'll have to do something about it, won't you?'

By such means, Grzimek raised money for research all over the world, to buy light aircraft for parks and for rescue operations. I have seen the logo of the Frankfurt Zoological Society alongside WWF's panda many times on vehicles and aircraft working for wildlife in remote parts of the world. Never a conventional man, in his seventies Bernhard Grzimek married Erika, his son Michael's widow. He died in 1988 at the age of 79, much mourned in wildlife circles.

6

The Animal Catchers

In the early years there was a limit to the sums of money the Wor
Wildlife Fund, the Frankfurt Zoological Society and other organ
sations could make available for capturing and relocating endanger
animals. There were other demands on their resources such as resear
and buying up land for reserves. Yet poaching was on the increase ar
human pressures on wildlife grew almost daily. Often the only soluti
was to move the threatened animals to a safer place. But first they h
to be caught.

As early as the 1950s it became clear that new capture techniqu
had to be found. The net, lasso and trap were no longer good enough
sufficiently safe. The tool that emerged was the hypodermic syrin
that could be fired from a gun at the target animal without endangeri
its life. The development and perfecting of this technique, usual
referred to as 'darting' or 'immobilisation', is a fascinating succe
story.

First in the weaponry field was the Palmer Chemical and Equipme
Company of Douglasville, Georgia. In the mid–1950s they came
with the Palmer Cap-Chur gun, a smooth-bored weapon rather like
20-gauge shotgun. The Grzimeks used an early model on the Sere
geti. It was powered by carbon dioxide compressed in two sm
cylinders. When the trigger was pulled, a puff of gas was released
project the 'bullet' – a hypodermic syringe. The shock of the dischar
mixed a tablet of carbide with water to generate acetylene gas whi
pushed forward the plunger of the syringe on impact, driving t
narcotic charge into the animal.

There were several snags with the early models. They had be
developed for use on captive animals in zoos or for veterinary pu
poses. For a running, jinking zebra or wildebeest, pursued by a captu
truck, usually a Land Rover, the range was not nearly long enoug

The darts were too sensitive. The jolting of the vehicle when driven flat-out across the bush frequently set off the interaction of carbide and water. No spare loaded syringes could therefore be carried. A fresh one had to be prepared for each shot. Also the generation of the acetylene often started the moment the syringe left the gun so that the narcotic was already oozing out of the needle while the dart was in flight.

Michael Grzimek took the gun to an instrument-maker in Frankfurt and suggested a number of modifications, including mechanism that activated the syringe plunger on impact. An improved compressed air system doubled the range of the weapon. Even then the Grzimeks were by no means sure about the type of drugs to use, let alone the quantities needed to put out the different species they proposed to mark for their study of the Serengeti migration.

At about the same time, pioneer work was being done with a older means of firing a dart. The crossbow was already enjoying a renaissance, largely in the United States, as a hunting weapon. In Uganda, Dr John Lock of the Pharmacological Department of Makerere College was experimenting with crossbows made from the leaves of old car springs. Later, commercially made crossbows became an accepted alternative to dart guns though they proved awkward and bulky to use in the confined space of capture vehicles.

The production of the right weapon was a mechanical problem which was bound to be solved in the long run. By the 1960s efficient capture guns, powered by blank cartridges, or more often by carbon dioxide cylinders, were in general use. The perfection of effective and safe drugs, however, was a far more complex matter.

During the mid-1950s darters in the field had to depend to a large extent on guesswork. When darting zebra and wildebeest on the Serengeti, Bernhard Grzimek relied on his zoo and veterinary knowledge. He had already tested the drug nicotine salicylate on goats and found that they would tolerate up to 4.5 milligrams per kilogram of body weight. The first time the Grzimeks tried this drug on wildebeest they cut the dosage down to one third. After 8 hours, the animal was still 'out'. It was growing dark. They dared not leave the wildebeest as it would certainly be attacked by lions or hyenas. As it was, a hyena did advance during the night, catching the drugged animal by the tail, and had to be driven off. At last, as the sun was rising, the wildebeest staggered to its feet and rejoined the herd. The Grzimeks couldn't afford to wait all night by the side of every animal they darted, so they cut the dose drastically, eventually discovering the correct shot to put wildebeest out long enough for them to complete their work. This usually consisted of marking it with a coloured plastic collar. The dose was about one third of that required for a goat! They also found that the amount of drug that would put out a large animal like a wildebeest had hardly any effect on the diminutive and lively Thomson's gazelle. Practically every species required a different treatment.

The pioneer and ultimate expert in this field was a South African, Dr Toni Harthoorn of the Faculty of Veterinary Science of Markerere College, Uganda. With John Lock, he worked on two types of immobilising drugs. The first were neuromuscular blockers such as succinycholine. These paralyse the animal but leave it fully conscious. They did, however, cause several fatalities at Kariba. Later, centrally acting drugs were developed. These affect the central nervous system, producing anything from anaesthesia to tranquillisation depending on the condition of the animal, the dosage and the circumstances of the darting.

The centrally acting drug that had evolved from experiments made in 1960 was called thiambutene. Three years later, a more powerful and even safer drug, Etorphine, usually known as M99, made the capture of large wild animals almost a routine affair. Later still, another product called Fentanyl emerged from the labs. When used in combination with various tranquillisers, it put rhinos and even elephants into a trance-like state in which they could actually be led into their crates. With the aid of Fentanyl, field-workers found they could lean ladders against the flanks of tranquillised elephants in order to take measurements. Wild buffalo became so tractable they could be ridden towards their loading crates. Tranquillised leopards were moved in open trucks, sitting up between their captors, as happy as dogs going for a ride with their masters. Mortalities, which were as high as 10 per cent with the early drugs, were virtually eliminated.

The pioneer darters, who included the American biologist Lee Talbot working on the Serengeti, soon found, however, that the problems of darting animals did not end when the hypodermic successfully hit its target. The trouble with centrally acting drugs was that the animal often ran a long way, sometimes as far as half a mile, before the drug took full effect. Each species tended to react in its own way after the dart had struck home. Plains animals such as zebra and wildebeest seldom ran very far. Even if they did, on the open savannah they were rarely out of sight. Bush-dwelling animals like rhino, kudu, roan antelope and even eland, the largest of all the antelope, instinctively made for dense cover. Occasionally, the strange side-effects of centrally acting drugs actually helped the capture team. The darted animal sometimes walked aimlessly in circles. Toni Harthoorn recalls the case of a lightly drugged elephant that walked rapidly in a mile circle, passing the capture team's truck three times before coming to a halt close by. In the elephant's case the under-drugging was accidental, probably due to a malfunction in the dart.

It is fairly difficult to lose a partially drugged elephant but a rhino can disappear when it runs half a mile into thick thorn scrub before it collapses. If it can't be found quickly and the antidote injected, then there is a real chance that the animal will die. These days, helicopters are often used to follow a darted animal, circling over the point of collapse or calling up the capture team by radio. But helicopters, which are also used for darting, are expensive to operate. Perhaps the ideal following instrument is the simplest one of all – the horse. Unfortunately, because of the tsetse fly, horses can only be used in a few areas in Africa. In Natal, for instance, with the tsetse fly absent, rangers can make their patrols on horseback. Since the 1960s, the Natal parks of Hluhuwe and Umfolozi have, due to protection in the comparatively small area of these two parks, had a surplus of the southern race of the white rhino. Many of these have been caught and transferred to other African parks and to zoos all over the world. When capturing their rhinos, the Natal parks used two mounted rangers to follow the darted animals. If the rhino ran into dense cover the riders split, each taking one side of a patch of thick thorn scrub and meeting at the end. This lessened the risk of the rhino breaking out sideways without anyone being the wiser. The horses could also cross ravines and thread their way through rocks that would have defeated a vehicle. The horses made less noise than a capture truck and were far less alarming. Another advantage was that they gave the rangers a raised viewpoint. When the riders reached the darted animal, one returned to report back to the catching team while the other stayed with the rhino. Both riders carried syringe kits and antidote so that emergency treatment could be given, if needed, before the main team arrived.

The methods used to approach animals for darting are many and various. Despite its disadvantages, a four-wheel-drive vehicle is the most common one. In dense bush or forest the job has to be done, often at considerable risk, on foot. In the Arctic, polar bears on the pack ice have been darted from the deck of a ship. On another occasion two light aircraft were used. One landed the darter on the ice while the other remained airborne to drive the bear towards him. Hippos have been darted from boats, rafts and, in one case from a road-grader.

As early as the rescue at Kariba, capture teams were learning that the aftercare of the caught animals was vital to their survival. With the development of the new drugs much more was learned about this aspect of darting. During the Natal operation not one of the 100 rhinos caught was lost as a result of the drugs or antidotes used. The only mortalities were due to crating or loading accidents, or to disease that developed during the acclimatisation period in the holding pens. Soon many parks had their own capture officers and specialised capture teams. Information was freely exchanged. As a result, each species and its aftercare became a text book case. Here are some of the standard procedures that evolved.

With the exception of elephants who are simply too large and too heavy, most drugged animals are best placed on their briskets, or breasts. With ruminants, this stops regurgitation and helps the release of gases. When deer and antelope have been feeding on fresh grazing they are very likely to regurgitate their last meal or to suffer from bloat.

Adult elephants can't survive long when resting on their chests. Twenty minutes is the absolute maximum. After the scientific work, maybe the placing of radio collars or perhaps ear-tagging has been carried out, they must be rolled over onto one flank. The best way to do this is to loop a rope round one tusk and then pass it over the top of the head. If the elephant is too heavy to be pulled onto its side by manpower or by vehicle, it can often be persuaded to roll over by rocking. Elephants are also subject to hypothermia. They are too heavy to be moved into the shade, so darting is usually done before the day gets too hot. Even so, dousing with water is essential to keep down body temperature. If elephants show signs of distress it isn't wise to aid respiration by giving small amounts of antidote. This is quite safe with other animals, but once an elephant gets back on its feet, thanks to small shots of antidote, there isn't very much you can do to control the reots of antidote, there isn't very much you can do to control the rest of the operation!

First aid for a drugged animal is more complicated than for an unconscious human being. With ruminants, the neck must be lifted and placed on a grass-filled sack. The head should be slightly above the level of the stomach. The mouth should be lower than the neck to allow for drainage of saliva. The animal is best laid on its right side to give the rumen the best chance of expanding. Human casualities are not bothered with this trouble. They may ruminate but they do not possess a rumen! Giraffe pose special problems. If the long-necked beast tries to rise while not still fully in control of its musculature, the head may crash to the ground with fatal results.

The glare of the tropical sun can do enormous damage to the eyes. A drugged lion wearing an eye mask, like those issued to air travellers on night flights, may look comical and undignified but, without such protection, it could easily become blind.

Temperature control is crucial with all drugged animals. Capture teams should carry a minimum of 20 litres of water and tarpaulins for rigging shelters from the sun. Tools should include axes and crowbars for freeing animals that have fallen into ravines, or become jammed between rocks or trees. A full first-aid kit for repairing and cleaning cuts and wounds, syringe wounds among them, should include antiseptic ointment that hides the smell of blood from predators and discourages insects.

Finally, when the last injection of antidote has been given, everyone in the team should withdraw except the man with the syringe. The animal should be watched from a distance but left to recover on its own. This way, the fear association with man is likely to be reduced and the animal will take its own time to get back on its feet. When it has done so, it must be given the best chance of being able to walk away at a gentle pace while it gets used to being upright again as the blood returns to its limbs.

If one dose of antidote doesn't do the trick, then half an hour should elapse before the next shot is given. Toni Harthoorn adds that if a rapid return to the upright is essential then there's nothing like a bucket of cold water in the face. 'Many animals,' he adds, not to my total surprise, 'are strongly stimulated by one or more fingers introduced into the anus.'

Toni Harthoorn is always humane in his approach to darting animals. In his book *The Chemical Capture of Animals*, on which I have drawn freely for technical information, he writes:

Chemical capture is essentially the capture of individuals and individuals have idiosyncrasies, differing sensibilities and varying degrees of resistance. This is plainly obvious to anyone who has ever reared a wild animal, be it a young elephant, rhinoceros or warthog or one of the spotted cats. Each has a definite personality.

Though the anaesthetic dart has made the capture and movement of wild animals almost routine, there are still some situations and some animals with which darting isn't possible. Then it is invariably a matter of returning to mechanical capture methods. This is what happened with the gemsbok in Namibia in 1969. The story of their capture, filmed by the German wildlife photographer Dieter Plage, became one of the most exciting half-hour 'Survival' films I have ever made. It was called *First Catch Your Unicorn* and was shown on television throughout the world. The unicorn of the title was the gemsbok (pronounce the 'g' as an 'h'). Otherwise known as the southern race of oryx. The unicorn refers to the fact that when early travellers first saw this pony-sized antelope they believed they were looking at a mythical beast. Seen sideways on, the two long straight horns can look like *one* long straight horn though, of course, the illusion is destroyed directly the animal moves.

The gemsbok that were to be captured lived in the pro-Namib, the arid stony region that borders the great Namib desert, the oldest desert in the world. Many of its dunes are over 1,000 feet high. It stretches 500 miles southward from the Kuiseb River canyon to the Orange River, the border with South Africa. The gemsboks' only crime was that they were competing for grazing with the farmers' valuable karakul sheep. Karakul are the sources of beaver lamb fur for coats, so Karakal farming is an important industry in a country not over-endowed with means of earning foreign currency.

It should have been perfectly possible to have darted the gemsbok. There was, however, one factor that made this inadvisable. In the contorted dune country of the pro-Namib it would have been only too easy to lose a drugged gemsbok. Apart from that, a darted animal was highly likely to run into terrain where a vehicle could not follow. So, the Department of Nature Conservation and Tourism which is responsible for Namibia's national parks decided on a mechanical catch. The ranger put in charge was a capture expert called Peter Flanaghan.

I wouldn't call Flanaghan's unicorn capture typical of all such mechanical operations. It does, however, illustrate the fact that when capturing and moving wild animals, drugs are not always the complete answer. Flanaghan's plan was to chase the gemsbok across the flatter and firmer parts of their range and then grab them by their luxuriant, horse-like tails until they slowed down sufficiently to be given a hand-administered shot of tranquilliser. In captures of this sort, drugs are often given as a back-up either to immobilise the animal or to calm it down or both.

Flanaghan was a delightfully eccentric if exasperating man to work with and particularly to film. Among his more amiable eccentricities was a tendency to whip out a Smith and Wesson .44 revolver and blast an offending fly off the aluminium camp table on which he and Dieter Plage ate. He insisted on his daily hip bath in this waterless country and, since he liked to enjoy a good view from his tub, had his African capture team carry his bath up to the top of a 500-foot dune. They took it very good-naturedly, no doubt thinking themselves lucky the *bwana* hadn't opted for one of the 1,000-foot dunes, of which there were plenty about.

From a filming point of view, the thing about Flanaghan that drove Dieter Plage close to madness was that he never wore the same clothes for more than a few hours at a time. Since film sequences are made by joining lots of shots together, Flanaghan sometimes appeared to change from bush hat to crash helmet in mid-chase. Each evening Flanaghan would promise to turn out next morning in the clothes he had worn when filming stopped. It made no difference. Dieter's only hope was to shoot enough chases in different turn-outs and hope that the film editor and I would be able to piece together enough sartorially matching sequences and that, if we couldn't, then the action would be thrilling enough to deceive the viewer's eye. On the whole, I think we succeeded. The gemsbok capture certainly did. Around 25 animals were caught and moved to an area where they would no longer be a target for the karakul farmers' rifles. Their new home was some 120 kilometres distant, far enough away to suppress any urge they might have had to return to their former home range, always a risk with translocated animals.

The actual method of capture was surprisingly simple. Built onto the front of the capture vehicle, in this case a Land Rover, was a platform made of tubular steel bars. The African catcher hung on to this for dear life until Flanaghan brought the vehicle, in a great cloud of red Namib dust, alongside the gemsbok, travelling between 25 and 30 mph. Once a handful of tail had been grabbed, Flanaghan slowed down. So, surprisingly, did the gemsbok allowing the tranquillisers to be injected and lengths of rubber hose pipe to be slipped over the tips of its horns to lessen the risk of damage to itself or the catchers. The captive was then transferred to a holding pen to settle down for about a fortnight before being moved to its new home by road.

*

There is one classic mechanical catching story that perfectly demonstrates how methods of capture and transportation have to be adapted to the animal and circumstances in question. As with the gemsbok, the movement, once capture had been completed, would not have been possible without the use of tranquillising drugs. The subjects this time were baboons, not just any baboons but the most famous in Africa, the members of the troop known as the Pumphouse Gang.

Baboons are one primate still in plentiful supply over much of Africa. They are not a particularly popular species of monkey. Many people find their presence and habits, even their appearance, somewhat unattractive. This is perhaps because most people who come in contact with baboons don't understand them. Baboons live in troops. Their social organisation inside those troops is something that *Homo sapiens* should envy and, in some respects, even emulate. We have only come to understand this social structure recently and largely through the work of an American Associate Professor of Anthropology at the University of California, San Diego, Dr Shirley Strum.

Before it became necessary to move it, the Gang lived on the 45,000-acre Kakopey Ranch, 75 miles north of Nairobi in Kenya. It took its name from a small pumphouse in the middle of the troop's home range. Kakopey is where Shirley Strum began her study of the troop in 1972 at the age of twenty-six. Her investigation was at first anthropological rather than primatological. By understanding the highly complicated social life of baboons she hoped to be able to obtain fresh insights into the behaviour of early man. As might have been expected, she found she was studying baboon behaviour primarily, though possibly shedding some light on early human behaviour in the process. Among the things she and her assistants learned was that baboons were a matriarchy and that they weren't governed by the macho males, as had previously been thought. The Pumphouse Gang became particularly famous among zoologists after Shirley Strum discovered that some members of the troop had become skilled at killing and eating the young of Thomson's gazelle, a hitherto unsuspected carnivorous trait among baboons.

All went well with Professor Strum's study until the end of the 1970s. Then the Gang developed the unfortunate habit of raiding local *shambas* for the small-holders' crops, notably maize. Raiding didn't stop there. Across the main road at Gilgil lay an army camp. The baboons found a great deal to attract them in the camp's rubbish dumps. The wives of the Kenyan troops became frightened of what the baboons might do to them or their children. Shirley Strum's study was obviously going to be endangered, as were the baboons, if something wasn't done soon. Baboon characters she had studied for eight years were suddenly no longer there. They had been shot by irate farmers.

Shirley Strum tried a reasonable approach with farmers and army both of whom were fairly reasonable in return. The only ones who weren't were the Pumphouse Gang. Attempts to scare the baboons away didn't work. Baboons don't scare easily. When 15 animals had been shot, Shirley and her co-workers started to look for another home for the Gang. It was far from easy. First she had to find a farmer who was willing to have another troop of baboons on his land. Then the habitat had to be right both for the baboons and for her study. For the latter there had to be open savannah. She and her assistants had so habituated the Gang to their presence that all their field work was done on foot among the troop. Rocky country or heavy scrub would make this sort of day-to-day observation very difficult if not impossible. At last, 80 miles to the north-east, outside the Rift Valley and within sight of Mount Kenya, she found what she was seeking at Chololo Ranch. Not only was there a willing rancher but permanent water, an essential for the baboons, and roosting cliffs similar to those in which the troop had slept at Kakopey. The search had taken over a year.

The Pumphouse Gang now numbered 98. If the capture was to succeed the whole Gang had to be caught in one fell swoop. It was the first time anything like this had been attempted. There were very good reasons for doing so. For one thing, it would be extremely hard to round up any strays missed in the first catch. Then, any that escaped permanently would join other troops on Kakopey Ranch – home to about 1,000 baboons all told – and teach them the art of crop raiding.

Shirley contacted the Institute of Primate Research in Nairobi. They confirmed what she already knew, that it would be impossible to catch a whole troop of baboons by darting them. They would have to be trapped. Cage traps were set up on a hilltop inside the Gang's home range. The metal doors, which worked on a drop principle, were wired up so that they could not fall and the traps baited with the baboons' favourite food – maize. Within a few days the baboons turned up in troop formation, entered the cages and helped themselves gratefully to the free hand-out. This went on for a fortnight. The bait was always placed on a wooden platform at the top of the cage so that the animal would have to stand up to get it. By doing so it would keep its tail out of harm's way when the door of the trap eventually fell.

When the chosen day for the catch came, Shirley and her helpers were in position before dawn, just out of sight, watching the traps. For the first time the baboons were late. An hour went by and then, when it seemed as though the baboons had somehow become suspicious, the troop appeared over the crest in full formation. The wires had, of course, now been removed from the mechanism and when the first door fell with a clang Shirley half expected to see the rest flee in panic. Nothing of the sort happened. Greed overcame caution. Within half an hour 97 baboons were behind bars. The solitary escapee was successfully rounded up shortly afterwards.

Once they were safely inside the traps, the baboons were given a shot of tranquilliser with a hyperdermic inserted through the bars. A medical reception area had been set up on the ranch nearby. Shirley's team had never been able to check the physical condition of the Pumphouse Gang before. Blood samples were taken, thorough checks made on heart and weight, and the Gang found to be generally in excellent shape. Throughout this examination baboon babies were tied to their unconscious mothers with string, not that there was any risk of

Shirley Strum's team, or indeed the baboon mothers, mixing up the babies. The tethering procedure was simply for the benefit of helpers from the Institute of Primate Research who were unfamiliar with the troop. In addition to these routine checks, a few baboons were fitted with a radio collar for tracking by telemetry after release.

Loading started before dawn next day to take advantage of the cooler air. Ahead lay a 145-mile journey over winding roads, so stress had to be kept to a minimum. When they arrived at Chololo, six hours later, the trucks carrying the females and young took a different route from those containing the adult males. The females would be released just before sundown close to the roosting cliffs. The males, unloaded some distance apart, would remain in their cages for two or three days more to give the females and juveniles time to settle down. Before the females were released they were given food and water to see them safely through the night and to prevent them wandering. When the cages were opened, the females and young made straight for the roosting cliffs. Three evenings later the males were allowed to join them.

Two or three anxious days followed for Shirley Strum and her research assistant Mary O'Bryan and Hudson, her Kenyan field worker. The radio collars fitted to the selected baboons were capable of transmitting a signal over 30 miles but, if the wearers were hidden in a gulley or fold in the cliffs, it might be difficult to pick up a signal at all.

Within a week it was clear that the Pumphouse Gang had settled down in its new home and was as approachable as ever by Shirley Strum and her assistants. The only anxiety was over feeding. Chololo is much drier country than Kakopey so the question was: would the Gang adapt to feeding on some of the different vegetation found there? To tide them over any initial difficulty, a truck-load of food had been brought to supplement their wild feeding. It wasn't needed for very long. Moving day for the Pumphouse Gang, an operation unique in the annals of wild animal translocation, had gone without a hitch.

The Pumphouse Gang settled down well in their new home. However, for reasons known only to baboons, they decided Chololo wasn't exactly what they were looking for and found better foraging territory slightly to the east where they are still being successfully studied by Shirley Strum and her assistants.

*

When it comes to mechanical capture methods, one technique stands out above all others. Its main use is with herd animals. It was perfected by Jan Oelofse, a South African, when he was Chief Capture Officer of the Natal Parks Board. In the late 1960s and early 1970s the Natal Parks had a number of surplus plains animals which they wished to move to other reserves and parks. Oelofse's basic problem lay in the terrain of Umfolozi and Hluhuwe. Much of the areas frequented by zebra and wildebeest is too mountainous and heavily treed to allow for capture involving vehicle chases. At first Oelofse tried catching his herd animals by driving them into nets. Although he caught a fair number, the casualties caused by hitting nets and becoming entangled were far too high to be acceptable.

Oelofse recalls spending many sleepless nights trying to come up with a better solution. If only, he thought, he could find a light, opaque, curtain-like material which appeared to be a solid wall into which the animals would not run. He decided to experiment with woven plastic. Early trials suggested that he had found the answer and that, with the aid of a helicopter to drive them, he would be able to capture a large number of plains game in a very short time. He eventually came up with a pen that required 1,600 yards of plastic and 3,200 yards of steel cable from which to suspend the plastic wall, the whole ending in a loading ramp leading up to a truck. Two plastic gates were to be drawn shut behind the animals as the chopper herded them further and further into the funnel.

The daily movements of a herd that was to be captured were first studied and the corral built upwind of them, preferably behind a ridge about 2 miles away. It helped, too, if the area contained a good many scattered bushes or trees to add to the deception. Four men stood ready by each plastic gate to draw it across behind the stampeding animals. The pilot, flying low, herded the animals towards the outer wall of the plastic. This was curved away at right angles to the main pens in order to funnel the herd in. As soon as the animals were within 200 yards of the gates, the chopper came in still lower to stampede them the last bit of the way. Experience showed that the chopper had to stay in the air until the gates had been drawn across, otherwise the animals were likely to break back and escape. The animals to be loaded, always of the same species, were then herded into the final loading pen by men walking forward slowly with a length of plastic sheeting stretched between them. Once the animals were inside the crush pen, a third gate was closed behind them. The captives, about 10 to a truck, were surprisingly easily persuaded to mount the ramp into the waiting transport. Oelofse found that it took an average of 15 minutes to select and load a group of animals and that the helicopter drive itself only took slightly longer.

In the first year, Oelofse's method caught and moved 3,500 animals including wildebeest, impala, zebra, nyala, kudu, warthog and waterbuck. Later, he was successful with buffalo and once captured a white rhino – by mistake. The rhino made no attempt to escape. On another occasion a lion jumped into the plastic pen and couldn't find its way out. All these captures were made without the use of drugs. Perhaps the most amazing thing was the willingness of the animals, provided they were of the same species, to travel together immediately after capture without fighting. What made this possible was the natural cohesion of creatures that belong to the same herd.

*

Not only helicopters but also light aircraft now play such a key part in so many saving operations that they have become, like the anaesthetic dart and gun, essential conservation tools (see Notes on The History and Use of Light Aircraft). In New Zealand red deer have been immobilised in difficult mountain terrain by a syringe fixed to a 12-foot pole which is wielded by a ranger perched in the open door of a chopper; a technique that calls for skilled low-level flying. A Colorado wildlife biolgist called Denney specialised in leaping from a helicopter onto the back of elk and deer slowed down by being chased into deep snow. By this terrifying means, Denney caught 78 elk and six deer in order to fit them with coloured neck bands for movement study. Normal capture accounted for three animals per hour. Denney's technique raised the rate to 11 per hour. In telling the story, Toni Harthoorn comments: 'This method should not be attempted casually'.

At the other extreme is the use of heavy air transport for moving wildlife. The most spectacular example I have come across was when making a 'Survival' film, again with Dieter Plage in Namibia, this time about the capture and translocation of a pocket of roan antelope threatened by poachers. Roan are one of the largest and most powerful antelope. In a normal situation they can be moved short distances in crates. The distance in this case was 600 miles from the Botswana border to Etosha National Park. Roan were once plentiful in Namibia. At the time of this rescue in 1978 it was reckoned that there were only 400 left.

With the aid of a helicopter, darting should have presenting few problems. The question remained: how to move the 70 or so roan that the parks aimed to catch across 600 miles of rough bush country? The only answer was a large transport aircraft. The obvious choice was a Hercules C 130, the workhorse not only of freight companies but of every air force in the world. The Hercules can lift enormous weights including tanks and vehicles. It had, however, never had a passenger list consisting of a number of large wild animals, any one of which was capable of kicking a hole in the side of the cargo bay. The Hercules is able to take off and land in remarkably small spaces. But in the middle of the African bush could any suitable clearing be found? Reconnaissance revealed that the dried up river-bed of the Khaudum River close to the catching area would just permit a landing and, with skill, a take-off fully laden with antelope.

As it turned out, the roan weren't at all easy to dart. As soon as they heard the chopper coming, they fled and hid in the thick bush and scrub along the banks of the Khaudum River. The pilot of the chopper, ex-RAF squadron leader David Todd, often had almost to brush the tops of the thorn scrub to drive them into the open.

The trickiest part of the operation was yet to come. When 74 roan had been captured and had settled down sufficiently in the holding pens to be moved, the C 130 was contacted by radio. The pilot took a number of close looks at his rock-strewn river-bed airstrip and then made his final approach. To stop in such a short space, he had to apply his brakes as soon as possible. The result of the touch-down was to lift a good part of the river-bed into the air. From a distance it seemed as though the Hercules had crashed in a cloud of yellow smoke. When the 'smoke' cleared there was the great plane, sitting safely but with only about 75 yards of 'runway' left.

The tranquillised roan were slid into the hold on loading pallets. Then their heads were secured by a loose length of rope fixed to an overhead rail, just in case they decided to come round in flight. When the time for take-off came, the pilot ran his engines up one by one so that the plane once again disappeared in a yellow dust cloud. On take-off he held the Hercules down for a heart-stopping length of time but eventually lifted off with less than 30 yards of runway left. Ian Hofmeyr, Etosha's vet and capture officer, of whom a great deal more later in this book, flew with his patients (Hofmeyr had also done the darting), administering small shots of tranquilliser in flight. All arrived safely in Etosha where they were off-loaded into acclimatisation pens and eventually released successfully into the park to breed.

★

Wildlife capture has come a very long way since those early desperate smash-and-grab operations at Kariba. In some cases it has become almost a time-and-motion study. The Natal Parks reckon that the time taken from darting to loading a crated white rhino on a truck for translocation averages 40 minutes.

There is no longer any insurmountable difficulty in capturing any animal for translocation or for scientific study. Invariably the reason for doing so arises because its needs have in some way come into conflict with those of man. The problem now is not so much how to capture wild animals but where to put them in order to ensure that they will thrive and multiply. If endangered animals need saving, even more, these days, does the habitat in which they can continue to exist. Unfortunately no dart guns or drugs can save rain forests or grasslands. Only man's goodwill and determination can come to the rescue in their case.

7

Hunters Aren't All Killers

Now the conservationists' techniques have improved, it is possible to save mammals that are in danger by moving at least some of them to areas of safety. The same, alas, is rarely true of birds. When it comes to saving birds there are basically two problems. The first and, in a way the easiest to deal with – though easy in this context is a comparative term – is the case of the resident or non-migratory bird. In this instance, it is the destruction of habitat – the reed beds, woodlands, heaths or marshes where the bird lives and breeds – that is almost invariably to blame.

A classic example is the case of the noisy scrub bird. The fact that this rather nondescript little bird continues to exist at all is due in large part to that most active conservationist, Prince Philip. During a visit to Australia for the Commonwealth Games in 1968 Prince Philip, who was at that time becoming more and more involved in conservation, happened to hear that this modest little bird was in danger of losing its last home. The woodland in which it nested, in fact its only nesting habitat, was about to be obliterated by the building of a new town on the south coast of Western Australia. Philip was able to put a little pressure on the authorities. It was at a time when Australia was waking up to the fact that it didn't have the best possible image for saving its wildlife. A few active conservationists like Vin Serventy were making this fact plain. The result of some fairly tactful lobbying was that the site for the new town was moved and the threatened songster was able to continue making its noise in the scrub to which nature had attached it.

It is by no means always as easy as that. It's even questionable whether a bird that is clinging on to existence by such a narrow margin (one suitable piece of forest left in the world) can continue to exist. Many people would argue that, within a few years, it is bound to go the way of the great auk, the labrador duck and the passenger pigeon, all of which have become extinct within the last 150 years. Many conservationists would argue that every effort should be made to save the bird. Others, perhaps more practical, would regard the scrub bird as a lost cause and put their efforts into more realistic acts of conservation.

It is hard not to sympathise with the save-it-at-any-price school of thought. The idea of allowing a creature to become extinct through neglect is, emotionally at least, unthinkable at this moment in time. Birds *have* been brought back from the edge of extinction, though for how long is another question. Perhaps the most dramatic example is the case of the Laysan teal.

Laysan is a small island in the Pacific 900 miles west of Honolulu. In the 1930s, a hurricane all but obliterated the wildlife on the island. US Fish and Wildlife wardens found that one nest of this little duck had survived with a clutch of eggs in it. The survival of the species depended entirely on the contents of that one nest. The eggs were taken away and put in an incubator. Most hatched out. In time there were enough descendants from this one clutch to return a breeding nucleus of Laysan teal to the island. There are about 70 breeding on a lake on Laysan now and many more in wildfowl collections around the world. This last-ditch saving operation has to be counted a success story. Whatever happens on Laysan now, there are enough of the species in wildfowl collections, including the Wildfowl Trust, to ensure its survival, though fertility rates among captive breeding birds are said to be falling. Should another hurricane wipe out the resident birds on Laysan there is no guarantee that the island could be successfully restocked with duck from wildfowl collections. The characteristics necessary for survival in the wild may well have been bred out of them in captivity.

Both noisy scrub bird and Laysan teal were endangered residents. The second bird conservation problem, that of species which migrate over large distances, is a far more complex one. It involves the co-operation of many people whose interests are not necessarily sympathetic to bird conservation.

The longest bird journey in the world is made annually by the Arctic tern that migrates 11,000 miles from the Antarctic to the Arctic tundra to nest. Fortunately for the tern it is not a hunter's quarry. This does not, of course, mean that it is free from danger. Its nesting habitat can still be disturbed. The food on which it relies to supply its journey and nesting energies, can be denied it by pollution or over-fishing. Nevertheless, it does not have to face the additional hazard of being shot at en route.

Birds that are good to eat or become a quarry, legitimate or otherwise of the hunter, face additional dangers. The classic case is that of the Bewick's swan, a protected species which nests around the coasts of the Kara Sea in Soviet Russia. The Russians are good conservationists. Even if they weren't, the swans are not likely to be disturbed on their tundra nesting grounds since these are a militarily sensitive area. There are almost certainly missile installations around the Kara Sea so no trigger-happy hunter is going to be allowed to wander around, peppering the swans with buckshot.

When they leave their nesting grounds in autumn, the Bewicks head south-west for Britain, where many of them spend their winter at the Wildfowl and Wetland Trust in Slimbridge, Gloucestershire and in Welney on the Ouse Washes of Cambridgeshire. There they enjoy full protection and receive large hand-outs of grain. What happens to them between the points of departure and arrival is largely beyond anyone's control. The Trust keeps detailed records of the returning swans which, fortunately, are individually recognisable by their face markings. Some swans have been returning faithfully with their devoted mates for years. Inevitably some fail to return, perhaps due to natural causes or unavoidable accidents such as hitting overhead power cables. However X-rays of swans caught for examination reveal that a large number have lead shot embedded in their bodies. Though the countries over which they fly on migration give them protection, nothing can protect them from the irresponsible man with the shotgun who does not care what he shoots at.

Despite this, as migrants go, the Bewicks are lucky birds. Conservation is on their side. Their more than 2,000-mile migration route takes them through Holland, Germany and Scandinavia where conservation is an active and established force. Not all migrants, especially the smaller birds, are so fortunate. Lack of size does not protect many of the songbirds who make a yearly migration, in some cases far longer than that of the Bewick swans' journey, from Africa to Europe and back again. Until, and if, they reach the comparative safety of northern Europe, they are constantly in danger. At the moment of writing the greatest risk is run by those birds using the western migration route up Africa and into Spain. Spain offers them sanctuary and full protection at such vital staging points as the Coto Danana and the marismas alongside the river Guadalquivir. Southern France offers sanctuary in the admittedly shrinking marshes of the Camargue. No doubt the migrants are shot for the pot as they continue north through these countries but that is a minor menace compared with what is happening in the interior of Africa. Here, in the region known as the Sahel, the

Sahara desert is moving south. The reasons are largely unknown. It may be due to climatic change, perhaps because we are at present in an inter-glacial period. As a result of the increasing aridity, what vegetation remains is being over-grazed by the resident and nomadic people of the region who thus unwittingly aid the southward spread of the desert. This should be seen first and foremost as a tragedy for the tribes that live in the Sahel. Where legitimate human needs conflict with those of wildlife, no sensible conservationist would claim that wildlife should take priority. In this case, though both humans and wildlife appear to be the victims of forces that are too immense and too little understood for a quick solution, or maybe any solution, to be found. It is easy to blame this, along with a good many other climatic changes, on the Greenhouse Effect. It may be that this is the reason but it will take many years of observation and research before anyone can be certain and by then, for the Sahel, the change may be irreversible. Purely in terms of wildlife conservation, the destruction of the Sahel is a disaster for the small migrants who have always used this route on their spring and autumn migrations. If Britain and northern Europe find themselves increasingly short of warblers and other delightful spring visitors, it will almost certainly be because these birds have been unable to overfly the southward-moving desert.

The small migrants who use the central and eastern end of the Mediterranean as air routes to their nesting grounds have long had to run the gauntlet of the netter and bird-limer who catch small birds for sale as food. Visit a southern European food market and it is still possible to see rows of songthrushes and robins on sticks offered as delicacies. It is estimated that in France alone 13 million thrushes of five species are taken each year for food. Southern European countries, not all of whom are members of the EEC, are said to account for 900 million bird deaths a year, many of them by illegal methods such as liming and netting. Legislation, enforcement of the law and, above all, education are the only factors that can alter this state of affairs. Maybe the Euro-Parliament in Brussels can do something about its member nations, but it seems fairly doubtful. Currently, the EEC nations are finding it hard enough to agree policies about levels of acid rain pollution and dumping of dangerous wastes in the North Sea. The chances of Euro law-makers agreeing on bird conservation policies that meet the needs of all member countries seem extremely slim if only because each has different needs and situations. At this moment, the EEC is seeking to impose a close season on Britain for magpies when she has a plague of these birds. There are probably as many magpies in Britain as songbirds caught by the bird-limers of Cyprus. The only way a balanced protectionist policy can evolve for Europe is by constant lobbying and pressure by well-briefed Euro MPs from countries which, like Britain, see wildlife conservation as a priority.

The odds appear heavily stacked against the co-operation of different interests and nationalities along a lengthy migration route. Yet co-operation of this kind has already happened and succeeded in protecting wildfowl species other than the Bewick's swans. The story involves three nations, innumerable states and a whole army of axe-grinders. The most amazing thing, perhaps, is that a key part in this vast operation was played by the very people whom many blinkered conservationists like to cast as villains – the hunters, in this case American and Canadian waterfowl hunters. In Britain we call them wildfowlers. No matter, their quarry is the same in both cases – ducks and geese. I am a hunter and wildfowler myself so I must declare that I hold strong views about the valuable part the hunter (I use the word in the American sense) can and should play in conservation. This is not to argue, however, that the man with the shotgun or rifle is always blameless. Far from it. He certainly wasn't in the United States in the period between the two World Wars when America woke up to the fact that it was in danger of losing its immense population of ducks and geese. Just as the market gunner had helped to exterminate the passenger pigeon, so he now played his part in over-cropping another apparently limitless resource. It was the case of the buffalo all over again. The trouble lay largely in the fact that the ducks and geese of North America travel such immense distances on their spring and autumn migrations. They journey from the Arctic tundra down to the south of California and the Gulf Coast of Texas and even south again into Mexico. Each state and province has its own hunting regulations and close seasons which aren't always observed. Like the buffalo, the birds had been present in such uncountable numbers from the days when the early pioneer settlers first set eyes on them that it was impossible to believe that, whatever inroads were made into them, they could ever decrease.

In the early years of this century and right up to the early 1930s, shooting took place on the breeding grounds as well as around the nesting colonies. Not only was the annual increase being shot each year but the parent stock as well. In addition, the birds' general movements were still a mystery. They appeared seasonally from parts largely unknown and disappeared in a similar manner. It was not altogether surprising that sportsmen and market gunners took what they could get when they could get it. Moreover the hunters could now range further and further afield. The appearance of cheap early cars like the Model T Ford took the gunners to places they could not easily have reached before. So far the hunter's record is, admittedly, a black one.

Fortunately, there were enough hunter-conservationists who could see the way things were going and who were willing to advise on, and help form, legislation. The first big step came in 1916 when the USA and Britain, on behalf of Canada, signed a Migratory Birds Convention which put the Canadian Government squarely into the business of wildlife management for the first time. Both signatory governments now had to draw up laws affecting the shooting of waterfowl throughout their domains, no easy task in view of the entrenched attitudes of states and individual hunters along the birds' migratory routes. In Missouri there was even a case where the state challenged the rights of the US government's enforcement officer. The Supreme Court ruled in favour of the latter in a landmark decision by Justice Oliver Wendell Holmes. Missouri had claimed the exclusive right to kill and sell the waterfowl that arrives in its territory. Justice Holmes' summing up was a classic one:

> The whole foundation of the state's rights is the presence within their jurisdiction of birds that yesterday had not arrived, tomorrow may be in another state, and in a week a thousand miles away ... To put the claim of the state upon title is to lean upon a slender reed.

History does not record whether the good judge was a hunter but he certainly understood ducks and geese.

Despite new and enforceable legislation that defined the different seasons in which migratory fowl could be harvested in each state through which they passed, the numbers of ducks and geese continued to decrease at an alarming rate. Now that indiscriminate shooting had largely been curtailed, another reason for the fall in population had to be found. This was the moment at which the enlightened self-interest of the hunters began to play a leading role. For the first time, as the result of attaching numbered bands or leg rings to birds that had been captured and then released, the pattern of waterfowl migration was beginning to be understood. The great American bird artist John James Audubon is credited with the first successful banding of birds to study their movements. In 1803 he attached silver wires to the legs of a pair of eastern phoebes which returned to him the following year. The technique of banding migratory birds was well established in North America by the late 1920s (see Notes on The Banding of Wildfowl). By 1929 over 400,000 birds had been banded in Canada and the United

States. The recoveries of ducks and geese bearing leg rings had shown beyond doubt that there were four main flyways along which the birds travelled from breeding grounds in the far north to summer resting and feeding grounds in the south. These were known as the Pacific, Central, Mississippi and Atlantic flyways. In the 1920s a beginning was made by Congress to provide staging grounds for the birds along these flyways by creating National Refuges, a system which had been given its start in 1913 when President Roosevelt set up the first National Refuge at Pelican Island off the coast of Florida. Congress passed acts establishing the Upper Mississippi River Wildlife and Fish Refuge in 1924 and the Bear River Migratory Bird Refuge in 1929. The Migratory Bird Conservation Act, passed in 1929, allotted nearly $8 million for the purchase or lease of other waterfowl refuges along the flyways. Still the duck and goose populations fell.

A natural and apparently obvious remedy was to limit the hunting seasons. Between 1927 and 1930 the open seasons were changed three times, ending in a mere 30-day season in 1931. In the neighbouring states of Missouri, Illinois, Indiana and Kentucky, four different seasons were fixed by Federal authority. At this point the waterfowl hunters or anyway, the informed section of them, had had enough. A foundation called More Game Birds in America appeared on the scene backed by rich hunters who were willing to spend money on research, and to work with the Federal and Canadian authorities to put scientists and equipment into the field in order to find out what was the real cause of the decline. If over-shooting was to blame, then so be it, but, both Federal and privately funded flyway biologists, as well as hunters, already suspected that there was a lot more to it.

The crisis deepened with the great drought that struck America in the early 1930s creating dustbowls in the central states and the prairie provinces of Canada, the very places where the duck bred. Moreover it soon became clear that many of the so-called potholes in these areas had been filled in as early as the First World War and many, many more during the Second World War to provide more space for growing wheat. These potholes are the product of advancing and retreating glaciers during the last ice age. The pothole country covers about 300,000 square miles in south central Canada and the north central United States. It stretches from Edmonton in Alberta, east to Prince Albert in Saskatchewan, and to Winnipeg in Manitoba and across the United States border into the western parts of Minnesota and South Dakota. This stretch of prairie averages 300 miles in width and is around 1,000 miles in length. From a high altitude aerial reconnaissance plane, this random pattern of potholes resembles a First World

75

War battlefield after heavy rain has filled the shell craters. As on a battlefield, there is no order to the pattern. A square mile of prairie may contain 100 potholes or five. The main source of water for these potholes and lakes is snow-melt. However the natural system that keeps them filled with water in a good year and dries out many of them in a bad one is extremely complicated. It takes little to upset the water supply. In recent years farming has greatly changed the number and nature of the potholes to bring more land under cultivation. Though this area produces one fifth of the duck population of North America, the eco-system is a very fragile one. Three adjacent potholes may each produce something different a duck species needs; say, nesting cover, plant food and insect food for the ducklings. Obliterate one of the three and you have upset the system. In the late 1930s, drought plus drainage had produced the worst crisis the waterfowl population had ever faced. The birds had no doubt survived more severe droughts before and in time recovered their numbers. But now – and it has become an increasingly familiar situation – the added pressures imposed by man had tipped the scales, possibly irreversibly.

It was at this point that Ducks Unlimited appeared on the scene. The organisation of hunters out of which it grew, More Gamebirds in America, had conducted privately funded research that made it clear that if the prairie wetlands, notably in Canada, weren't restored, the waterfowl populations would decline permanently. The problem was that the laws of the United States prohibited spending public money for such purposes in a foreign country. Nor did Canada, then a British Dominion, have any legislation that allowed the tax-payers' money to be spent in this way. The only solution was to set up a privately funded organisation that could operate in Canada. Backed by businessmen, conservationists and hunters, Ducks Unlimited was also given strong government support. This manifested itself practically in the form of tax relief. A year later in 1938, the organisation of Ducks Unlimited, Canada, was completed. The first field work began that year. This is not to suggest that DU, as it is generally called, averted disaster single-handed. They could not have achieved what they did without the co-operation of federal and state, government and provincial wildlife services in both the United States and Canada. Perhaps their hardest task was to win farmers and irrigation authorities to their side. That they were able to do so is because they put into the field observers and experts, often duck hunters themselves, whose views were listened to and respected. They also had the clout of money that did not have to wait for legislation before it could be put to good use. With this money they employed hydrologists and engineers, since much of DU's work consisted of getting water to the right places and keeping it there when nesting waterfowl most needed it. It would also be fair to say that DU money made the light aircraft, an invaluable tool when surveying and taking population counts in remote areas, freely available to scientists and biologists working for many organisations in the battle to restore the pothole country.

What has DU achieved? They have raised and spent on their projects over $15 million. They have built over 750 new lakes and swamps and created networks of dykes and dams that have fed water back to innumerable smaller potholes. Though not primarily a research organisation, they annually band around a quarter of a million ducks and geese to determine distribution, flyway patterns and use of nesting grounds. They control water on more than 1 million acres in prime duck breeding territory. The shoreline around these waters is greater than the entire coastline of the United States. Ducks Unlimited coined a very apt phrase to describe their reclamation works on the prairies. They called them 'duck factories'.

Conservationists are only too aware that methods that suit one country are unacceptable in another. The restoration of the waterfowl population of North America could almost certainly only have happened in that continent. To begin with the two principal countries concerned not only shared the same land mass but also the same interest in protecting a jointly owned resource. Perhaps the most amazing fact is that their governments were so whole-heartedly behind the operation. It is unusual to find administrations determinedly on the side of conservation. Finally, there are few, if any, other countries in which the hunting element would be recognised as a powerful force for conservation.

The first initiative of the US government came from President Franklin D. Roosevelt (an extremely distant relative of Theodore Roosevelt). The years of the dramatic waterfowl decline largely coincided with the aftermath of the United States' great depression. Roosevelt's Public Works Administration was concerned with getting America's unemployed back to useful work. His plan put men to building great dams and other public projects. It also made millions of dollars available for wetland restoration. The money had to be spent in the belt hit by the drought, mainly in the Upper Mississippi Valley and the Great Plains. Congress was so pleased with the result that next year it voted to extend the programme with another $6 million. Under Roosevelt's early administration a bill was passed called the Migratory Bird Hunting Stamp Act (1934). Every duck hunter had to buy a stamp as his licence. The price started out at $1, today it is $12.50 and is bought by nearly two million hunters each year. To date, Duck Stamps have raised $331 million and purchased 220 refuges for waterfowl as well as 66,000 acres of waterfowl habitat. These are over and above the refuges established by Ducks Unlimited.

Unfortunately, a similar unification of bird protectionists' and shooters' interests has never come about in Britain, though excellent co-operation exists between the British Association for Shooting and Conservation (BASC) and the Wildfowl and Wetland Trust. In Britain, attitudes about field sports, including wildfowling, are far more polarised than they are in the United States, and there has certainly been no government money spent on wetland preservation, let alone reclamation. There is little doubt that birdlife in general, and wildfowl in particular, have been the losers of this failure to combine forces.

8

Massacre, Now!

Protecting migratory birds is difficult enough; protecting elephants is, in every sense, a far bigger problem. It is easy to forget that elephants migrate, too. They have always done so, using traditional routes, sometimes hundreds of miles long, as the dry and wet seasons force them to look for water and food. As the human population in under-developed countries grows – and it grows everywhere at an alarming rate – these traditional migration routes are denied to them by towns, villages, and farming, as well as by forestry and irrigation schemes.

One result of this human spread is that small concentrations of elephants become isolated in areas where the local population needs every square foot, of what is probably not very fertile soil, to grow subsistence crops. The elephants then become what is known as 'pocketed herds'. The pocket is invariably too small to shelter or feed them, and so they fall back on eating the farmer's crops which are defended, often with totally inadequate firearms. Many of the elephants are wounded and become man-killers. The wildlife authorities are then faced with two alternatives: wipe the pocketed herd out or find a way of trying to save the animals.

There is, however, a far larger problem, one that affects every elephant, African and Asian, still alive. At this very moment the greatest wildlife tragedy since the extermination of the buffalo in North America is taking place in Africa and to a lesser extent in Asia. The elephant has the misfortune to carry two overgrown teeth made of solid ivory. It has always been killed for these teeth, but until 15 years ago the killing, both by legitimate hunters and by so-called poachers, generally speaking has been kept within tolerable limits.

Now, for reasons that will be made clear, the African elephant is being slaughtered at such a rate that it is in real danger of following the trail taken a century earlier by the buffalo in North America. If the Asian elephant is slightly better off, it is only because the females do not carry ivory tusks. There are now very few large male Asian 'tuskers' left as they have all been shot to satisfy the Far Eastern market for ivory. In this desperate situation there are wardens, rangers and scientists willing to put their own lives at risk in the battle to save what is left of the world's elephants. I have had the privilege of knowing and working with some of these people during the course of making 'Survival' films. Before coming onto the larger problem of wholesale slaughter I will tell the story of two highly hazardous operations to save 'pocketed herds'.

Rwanda, the small African country that lies to the east of Zaire and to the west of Tanzania, is one of the most densely populated nations on earth. Its total area is only 10,000 square miles. Its population, which is still growing, is over four million. Every inch of land is cultivated to grow food. In 1975, Rwanda had only one herd of elephants left, numbering about 150 animals. This herd lived in a swamp right in the middle of one of the most heavily farmed areas. The herd was inevitably doomed. The farmers shot and snared the elephants to defend their crops. They also cut down the trees on which the elephants largely depended for food in order to make way for more cultivation.

After consultation with a firm of wildlife experts from Kenya, the President of Rwanda decided that the adult elephants must be shot, since they were under sentence of death from the farmers and could not be moved anyway, but an attempt was to be made to save the calves.

The next question was where to release them once they had been captured. Rwanda wished to retain the remnant of its elephants so there was no thought of transferring them to a neighbouring country. Rwanda has one national park, Kagera, where there were no adult elephants. Even if there had been, it was doubtful whether they would have adopted strange calves. There were, however, a number of lions which would certainly view the young elephants as a welcome addition to their menu.

A feature of the Parc Nationale Kagera is a 1½ mile-long headland that juts out into Lake Hago. The narrow neck of this headland could quite easily be sealed off with a strong electric fence which would effectively keep the lions out. In time, the elephants themselves might break this fence down but by then, with any luck, they would be big enough to defend themselves. As an additional precaution an attempt, largely unsuccessful, was made to drive the buffalo out of the peninsular. Failure was not however disastrous, for buffalo and elephant do not compete for food and the buffalo were unlikely to be aggressive to the young elephants, or vice versa. If the buffalo could have been persuaded to leave, the elephant calves would have had the advantage of being the only large mammals in the peninsular. As it turned out, no harm resulted.

Shooting the surviving adults of the swamp herd would be a bloody, unpleasant and possibly dangerous job but it presented no real difficulties. Catching and moving their offspring to a holding camp, where they would need at least three weeks to settle down before being shifted to Kagera, was fraught with problems. The move of a few miles to the holding camp at a place called Rwinzoka had to be made as quickly as possible, to reduce the risk of shock to very small calves recently deprived of their mothers' protection. Larger calves could be moved by water on the winding Nyabarongo River that ran alongside the swamp. A cataraman-type raft was built that would carry the bigger animals in a tubular steel cage. The smaller calves would have to be moved by air – and in a very unusual way. The first part of the operation, the shooting, revealed that half the adults and some of the larger calves were better out of the way. Many bore festering bullet wounds and some had old snare wire embedded in legs and trunks. All told, 106 elephants were shot. Once the killing was over the calves had to be captured as quickly as possible. In the dense papyrus swamp it would be quite easy to lose them. Kenyan vet Jerry Haig performed the darting. As has been shown, an animal can run a considerable distance after the dart has struck, so the team had to follow the darted youngster immediately. Once each young elephant had been immobilised it was tied to a stake to avoid the risk of it wandering off when recovering from the narcotic.

The encouraging thing about the capture was that quite a large number of the calves were big ones. With luck these would help to hold the herd together on release at Kagera. The first of the bigger elephants was loaded successfully on to the raft and sent downstream. Now came the unique part of the operation. A helicopter of the Rwanda Air Force hovered over the swamp and lowered its winch cable to the handlers on the ground. Heavily tranquillised, the first small baby, wrapped in a padded harness, was winched into the air and, still drugged out of its tiny pachydermatous mind, flown to the holding camp. What a young elephant feels like, even doped up to the tip of its trunk, when swinging like Dumbo several hundred feet in the air, is impossible to judge. Conservation often demands a high price from the animals it saves.

In fact, no serious after-effects seem to have been experienced by these unorthodox air travellers. The smallest of the babies, and the first to travel by helicopter, settled down the quickest of all. Baby elephants are notoriously hard to feed. Cows' milk is no good to them. Many of these were still being suckled at the time of capture. A mixture of mealie meal and powdered milk produced a fat content which they accepted with no harmful results. After three weeks of acclimatisation in the holding pens, 25 young elephants were taken by road to Kagera and released.

The heavy price of conservation operations of this kind is not always exacted on the animals. A great personal friend, the young American wildlife photographer Lee Lyon, who filmed the whole operation for 'Survival', was crushed to death by one of the larger calves seconds after it was set free. Normally such calves take a short time to get their bearings and then move away into the nearest cover. This one, quite unpredictably, charged and crushed Lee against the side of her truck and then knelt on her. Lee, a lovely girl of great talent and promise as a wildlife film-maker, came from California. She is buried in Kagera where the elephants she filmed are still thriving.

★

The second operation was even more unusual and may never be repeated. Again it concerned what has come to be known as a 'pocketed herd'. No-one had attempted to move fully-grown elephants before, nor had the method used by the capture team been tried previously. The year was 1979. This time it was an isolated herd of Asian elephants which were in urgent need of rescue. This herd lived in a coconut-growing area called Deduru-Oya in the beautiful, heavily populated island of Sri Lanka. A few years previously, the herd there was 150-strong. As the coconut plantations grew and became more productive, the number of elephants fell to 17. The conflict of interests was much the same as in Rwanda. The elephants lay up in cover during the day and came out at night to raid the coconut palms. Getting coconuts down from the top of a 30- or 40-foot palm is no problem for an elephant. It simply butts the trunk with its head and, if this fails, bulldozes the tree flat. The difference between the saving operation in Rwanda and this one was that practically all the Deduru-Oya elephants were fully grown adults weighing from 3 to 5 tonnes. As in Rwanda, the blame for the decimation of the herd cannot fairly be placed on the local farmers and cultivators who had to feed themselves or earn a living by selling their crops. If the blame lay anywhere, it was with those who allowed agriculture to spring up piecemeal, without planning for the needs of both farmers and wildlife. This failure dates back to the time

In North America hunters must buy the Duck Stamp each year. To date, this licence has raised $331 million for wildfowl conservation. The design changes yearly.

Numbered leg rings enable conservationists to keep a check on wildfowl populations and movements – in this case a teal.

The elephant herds at Lake Manyara, Tanzania, came to trust Iain Douglas-Hamilton completely. This is the moment when a one-tusked elephant called Virgo greeted him after two years' absence in England.

Adult wild elephants have been translocated successfully only once – in Sri Lanka. Trained working elephants calm the captives and guide them into trucks.

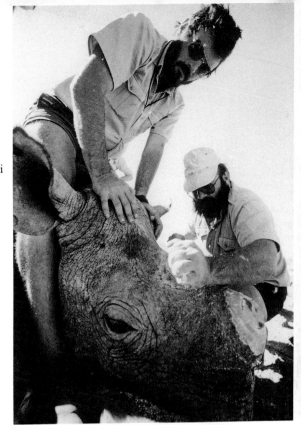

The last hope – wardens in Namibia remove the poachers' incentive to kill by sawing off the rhino's horn.

An expensive bonfire – President Moi of Kenya set fire to £1 million worth of illegal ivory as a gesture against poaching.

The simplest methods are
sometimes the best: Namibian
gemsbok are chased and grabbed
by the tail in preparation for
removal to a safer area.

Captured gemsbok are unloaded
into an acclimatisation pen to
settle down before release.

of British colonial rule, though it has been compounded since. Despite such failings Sri Lanka has remained a stronghold of the Asian elephant. A century ago the island, which is only 270 miles long by 130 wide, held 12,000 elephants. That was before the British planters started shooting them for sport and to protect tea and coffee estates up in the hills. The result of this was that elephants only survived in any numbers in the less fertile and dry lowlands. Nevertheless, at the time of the Deduru-Oya rescue in the late 1970s, there were still 4,000 Sri Lankan elephants left. That elephants existed in such numbers was largely due to the backing the President and Prime Minister gave to their then very able head of wildlife conservation, Lyn de Alwis, and his team.

A previous attempt had been made to translocate another pocketed herd but with little success, largely due to the inexperience of the darting team. What was called for at Deduru-Oya was an expert who would go on foot into the tangled jungle in which the elephants lay up during the daytime and dart at close range under the most difficult and dangerous conditions. Dieter Plage, the West German wildlife camera-man, whose adventures in the Namib Desert when capturing gemsbok have already been described, suggested his friend Ian Hofmeyr, the chief vet and capture officer of Etosha National Park in Namibia. Hofmeyr, who had darted everything in Africa from ostriches to lions, was delighted with the suggestion and volunteered to come at his own expense.

This solved the darting side of the rescue. The next stage had never been attempted before. The capture team aimed to persuade their tranquillised adult captives to walk up a ramp into the trucks waiting to transport them to Wilpattu National Park, a journey that could take anything up to five hours. De Alwis and his team, however, had a secret weapon. In Sri Lanka there are a good many trained elephants used in forestry and other heavy lifting work. He would use these to calm his captives and persuade them into the trucks. It was, after all, only an adaptation of the methods used to pacify captured wild elephants in the early stages of their training. In Assam, where elephants were until recently caught for work in the forests, tame elephants called *koonkies* are used not only to chase the wild herds during the capture method known as the *mela* but to act as 'schoolmasters' during the breaking-in process. During this phase of training, the *koonkies* are positioned on either side of the trainee so that it learns the commands that the *mahout* gives. It was this technique that was to prove crucial to success at Deduru-Oya.

Darting in the thick jungle undergrowth surrounding the plantations at Deduru-Pya was a nightmare. Visibility was seldom more than 10 yards. Stalking elephants in the dense scrub was far more hazardous than anything Ian Hofmeyr had encountered in Africa. Fortunately he was able to rely on the skill of the Sri Lankan trackers, to whom these conditions were quite normal. They had not only to get him close to his quarry but find him a clear field of fire for each shot.

The first elephant went down straight away under the influence of the Belgian drug Car Fentanyl. Five of the first ten elephants darted were blind in one eye. All had shotgun wounds which had long gone septic. Not all the dartings were as easy as the first. A big tusker charged Dieter Plage while he was filming, knocked him flying and ran right over him, one forefoot treading on his shirt but without touching his body. The camera remained running all this time obtaining a weird shot of the bull's belly as it passed overhead. The villagers asked that the team concentrate on a rogue bull elephant who had been shot at so often that he was ready to kill on sight. 'Sight' turned out to be a misnomer. The rest of the herd was so protective of this rogue bull that the only way the trackers could get near him was to drive his companions away with thunderflashes. The reason for this protectiveness soon became clear. The darting went well but success ended there. The bull was riddled with buckshot and blind in both eyes. Small wonder he had turned man-killer. There was no choice but to destroy the animal.

While still under the influence of the Car Fentanyl, the captured elephants were sandwiched between the tame animals and led towards the loading ramps into the trucks. At first, the snag was that the *mahouts* riding the trained elephants just did not believe that it was going to work and were reluctant to bring their mounts in close enough, but gradually their confidence increased.

Thanks to the effectiveness of the drug, the journey to Wilpattu passed without incident. The first release took place at night in the hope that the elephants wouldn't wander too far in strange surroundings. Ian Hofmeyr gave the first elephant a very small shot of the tranquilliser and then the team guided it down the ramp from the truck by means of ropes. The elephant went peacefully into a light sleep from which it was aroused by a final shot of antidote in the ear. By then a large figure one had been painted on its backside in hard gloss paint so that the parks could keep a track of its movements for some time afterwards. Ten elephants were caught and released but one cow walked back 50 miles across country to Deduru-Oya. It took her four days. When she got there she met up again with Ian Hofmeyr who was darting the remainder of the herd and tried her best to kill him. She was almost certainly looking for her calf who was ill at the time of capture and was taken to Colombo Zoo for treatment.

There is a postscript to this story more tragic, even, than the death of Lee Lyon in Rwanda because it was a double tragedy. Not long after Ian Hofmeyr had returned to Etosha he was showing some friends round the national park in the capture truck that was his pride and joy. This truck had been designed by Ian to stand up to every strain imposed on it and its crew when pursuing zebra at 30 mph, darting elephants and travelling at speed across the most rugged terrain with which Africa can confront a vehicle. Ironically the accident happened on a park track. Ian pulled over to allow a supply lorry to pass. His nearside wheels slipped into a drainage ditch and the truck rolled onto its side, pitching the driver out onto his head and breaking his neck. Neither of his passengers suffered a scratch.

Worse followed in Sri Lanka. Early on in the Tamil rising, a raiding party of Tigers swept through Wilpattu National Park. Most of the guards were gunned down including those who had taken part in Deduru-Oya elephant rescue. The head tracker who had guided Ian Hofmeyr in the jungle while darting the pocketed herd was forced to direct the raiders out of the park. When they reached the exit they shot their guide and threw his body out on the road.

While researching this book I received a letter from Lyn de Alwis. Lyn is no longer head of the parks but writes from the office of the Chairman of the Asian Elephants Specialist Group. He says:

With regard to the fate of the elephants. The painted numbers enabled staff to note natural markings on the Deduru elephants thereby identifying them long after the paint had worn off. Up to seven elephants were regularly seen, but not as a herd. Eighteen months after release a ranger showed me a lone cow with a calf at heel three days in a row and only 4 miles from the first release point. Another identified sub-adult cow was often seen bathing about 5 miles from the second release point.

The Deduru elephant problem ended with our operation. There was no more trouble with plantation raiding which at least confirms that none returned after the famous cow (No 7) who tried to run down Ian. I am certain that she was the matriarch of the herd. When she was released after being darted for the second time she was set free so far north of Deduru that I doubt if even she could plot a second course back there. The fact that she was carrying a huge bullet in her head from Deduru plantation workers may have deterred her also. Of course, I could be wrong. That's all the update I can give you as there isn't a soul I could now consult. As you know, the one assistant ranger, Mr H. H. A. Bandara, who might have kept tabs on the situation was killed by terrorists in 1985.

★

It is difficult to feel the full impact of the slaughter that is now taking place among the world's remaining elephant herds unless you have had the experience of close contact with these most magnificent of animals and, indeed, with the people who are in the front-line of the battle to save what is left of them.

In 1973, I had the good fortune to work for a short time with a young man called Iain Douglas-Hamilton in Lake Manyara National Park, Tanzania. Iain had for several years previously been making a study of the 500 elephants the park then contained. His study covered family behaviour, population dynamics and the elephants' adaptation, in terms of food requirements and migrational needs, to the comparatively small area of the park. His ultimate aim was to make recommendations for enlarging the areas available to the herds. The remarkable feature of his work was that it was conducted almost entirely on foot. It is a comforting thing when rubbing shoulders with a wild elephant herd to have some kind of vehicle wrapped around you, even if it is an unreliable, open-topped Land Rover. Iain had such a vehicle. Its battered appearance was the direct result of interference by elephant, usually one that had, as is almost invariably the case, a past history of being shot at and probably wounded by farmers. One elephant in particular, a large cow whom he had code-named Sarah, had on one occasion objected to him darting a calf for research purposes and stuck her crossed tusks into the radiator, pushing Land Rover and Douglas-Hamilton backwards through the bush for a good 30 yards. Despite such experiences, Iain much preferred to conduct his researches on foot. He started out by believing that if he moved quietly and respectfully enough among one or two selected herds, the elephants in them would come to trust him and accept him. And so it turned out.

My part in the study was that of an observer of a different kind. I was there with Dieter Plage and Lee Lyon – it was the assignment before the one in which she met her death in Rwanda – to make a 'Survival' one-hour film about Iain and his elephant study. This was eventually called *The Family that Lives with Elephants*. For once, the title was no exaggeration. The 'Survival' team, of which my wife made the fourth member, shared the Douglas-Hamiltons' family life with the elephants and with one herd in particular. We had to get used to hob-nobbing with the herd ruled by a huge and intimidating matriarch, 'Boadicea', on the same intimate and close-quarter terms daily used by Iain and his wife Oria. It was always exciting and sometimes quite frightening.

I will cite just one extraordinary example of Iain's rapport with, and understanding of, elephants. When we joined the Douglas-Hamiltons in their camp in Lake Manyara National Park, Iain had only recently returned from spending two years in Cambridge where he had obtained his doctorate. He had therefore just resumed acquaintance with the elephants he had got to know so well and with Boadicea's herd in particular. During the four years he had worked in the park he had struck up a close friendship with one young female in this herd. Like all Iain's study subjects she had been given a name, 'Virgo'. She was easily distinguishable. She was the only elephant in this herd that had one tusk. I was with Iain when he renewed acquaintance with her after his two-year absence. We had made contact with Boadicea's herd and the great matriarch had put in her enormously impressive threat charge possibly because there were strangers present. Iain knew that Virgo must be somewhere around and walked up the track calling her by name. After a few minutes Virgo emerged from thick scrub and approached Iain cautiously. He stood quite still in the middle of the track and slowly raised one arm. Virgo advanced carefully, as if not quite believing her eyes, and then placed the tip of her trunk against Iain's hand. Later, during the course of making our film, Iain and Oria would take their two small daughters Saba and Dudu to meet Virgo who extended the same courtesy and gentleness to them. Little wonder, then, that Iain Douglas-Hamilton later became a central figure in the fight to save the African elephant.

In the seventeen years that have passed since we worked together in Manyara, the elephant population of Africa has declined from an estimated 1½ million to perhaps 600,000. By the time you read this I have little doubt the total will have fallen again. At the time of writing 100,000 are still being killed annually. Many of the facts I now give concerning this disaster have been collected and researched by Iain Douglas-Hamilton, though, of course there have been many other workers in the field.

There is only one real cause of the disaster – poaching. This is no longer casual poaching by small opportunist bands of African hunters, but slaughter on the scale of an organised, though totally illegal, industry. So why has poaching for ivory, which has always been a fact of African life, escalated so greatly during the last decade? The scale of that escalation can be judged by comparing the population figures in some of the main elephant producing countries over less than a decade.

	1979	1987
Kenya	65,000	23,000
Uganda	6,000	2,300
Zaire	370,000	195,000
Tanzania	316,000	85,000
Zambia	150,000	41,000

The figures in the right-hand column have fallen a great deal further since the 1987 estimate was made. For example, by 1990 Kenya was reckoned to have only 10,000 elephants left. So the same question again: why the vastly accelerated rate of slaughter?

One reason, of course, has to be the rising price of ivory on both the black and legitimate markets during those years. Tusks selling at £35 per kilogram in Central Africa fetched £250 per kilogram in Hong Kong. Why the price should have risen so steeply in the past ten years no economist can fully explain. The most likely reason is that those who bought ivory saw it as a safe investment in a time of high inflation. Whatever the economic causes of the Great Slaughter it is the availability of modern repeating weapons that has made the poachers' work easy. I am indebted to Iain Douglas-Hamilton's excellent analysis in *Oryx* for illustrations of how such weapons as AK 47s have become the standard arms of highly organised poaching gangs.

Between 1971 and 1980, arms imports to Africa increased from US $500 million to $4,500 million. Armed forces in Central Africa during the same period increased from 141,000 to 441,000. Somalia armed in the early 1970s to prepare for the Ogaden war so Ethiopia had to keep pace. The same thing happened in East Africa. Amin armed in Uganda so Tanzania and Kenya felt they had to do the same. The question remains, how did so many of the arms with which these forces were equipped find their way into the hands of poachers?

In Uganda and the Sudan soldiers and poachers were sometimes one and the same people. Poorly armed and outnumbered park rangers could do nothing to stop them. Weapons were, in addition, lost, stolen or sold. Sometimes the ivory dealers gave guns to villagers and then paid them for what they shot. The collapse of the Idi Amin regime in Uganda was one of the main sources of automatic weapons. Iain Douglas-Hamilton describes to perfection in *Oryx* the outcome of Amin's weakening power. As Amin lost his grip on the wild northern region of Uganda called Karamoja, the warlike tribes that live there, known collectively as the Karamojong, took matters into their own hands. The national sport of the five Karamojong clans is raiding each other and their neighbours, the Turkana, for cattle and women, but

principally cattle. The Matheniko clan saw their chance and attacked
the police barracks at Moroto, looting the armoury and carrying off
among other weaponry 12,500 automatic rifles and 1,500,000 rounds of
ammunition. In this they were helped by another clan, the Jieh, with
whom they divided some of the spoil. Metheniko and Jieh then went to
war on the remaining Karamojong tribes and accumulated large herds
of stolen cattle. Now the victimised tribes had to get arms or go under.
There were by then plenty of loose weapons around so it wasn't hard to
catch up with their enemies. The Karamojong now had more weapons
than even they needed so they sold some to the Toposa in the Sudan.
The disease spread into Kenya. The Turkana, the powerful Kenyan
tribe around the great lake now named after them (it used to be Lake
Rudolf) had to arm themselves against the Karamojong to the west.

In 1979 the troops of Idi Amin retreating northwards ahead of the
liberating army from Tanzania were only too anxious to get rid of
weapons and uniform to avoid capture and execution. They sold or
gave away their automatic weapons to villagers. Unfortunately their
line of retreat to West Nile Province from which many of them came lay
through Murchison Falls National Park. Hundreds of rifles came into
the hands of the local people in that area and so they began to poach,
too. The story was repeated almost everywhere since there was no
shortage of civil wars in Africa even as far south as Angola where
guerilla troops traded ivory for arms.

In only one country has war helped the elephant. After a civil war
that lasted from 1972 to 1980 and ended with the foundation of an
independent nation, Zimbabwe had more elephants than at any time
since 1940, even though wildlife management had largely to be
suspended during the war. The bush had simply become too dangerous
for poachers. They were liable to be attacked by either government or
guerilla troops or blown up by mines. In 1940 there were between
10,000 and 13,000 elephants in the area. Today the population is more
like 45,000. This means that Zimbabwe has a different kind of elephant
problem, similar to that in Murchison Falls, Uganda and Tsavo
National Park, Kenya in the 1960s – too many elephants damaging and
altering their habitat. In this situation Zimbabwe both culls the surplus
and permits hunting on licence. It follows from this that the country
has a steady supply of legitimate ivory.

I am only too aware that anything I write now about the elephant
crisis will soon be out of date. I can therefore only report events as they
are, and speculate on how they may be. In 1989 the media suddenly
became aware of the tragedy overtaking the African elephant as the
result of what it called the rush to obtain 'white gold'. Hardly a day

passed without at least one newspaper carrying a feature article on the subject or without television broadcasting a news report or a documentary. For the time being, at least, the elephant had supplanted the whale as the animal most deserving pity, sympathy and support from the general public. Long may such support last. It is excellent as far as it goes. As with the whale, the question is: how far can it go? In both cases, there is very little the public at large is able to do in a practical sense. Unless you are Japanese you are unlikely to use whale products, at least knowingly. Where elephants are concerned at least you can and should refuse to buy ivory. Public opinion is, of course, a powerful weapon in itself, as was proved by the whale crisis. It is, for instance, possible for a country to refuse to buy fish or other products from a nation that persists in flouting the standards set by the International Whaling Commission. There was the case of an American university that turned down a US \$1 million electron microscope made by the Japanese in favour of a more costly one from Europe as a protest against Japan's attitude to whaling.

With the elephant it is not so easy. The African countries that still have elephants are in need of economic aid not sanctions. Moreover, their governments in most cases are not the offenders. They almost invariably appreciate the value of their elephants, if only as a tourist attraction, and are in favour of not only preserving them but increasing their numbers.

The enemies of the elephant in Africa have to date been: (1) corrupt politicians and officials who have been taking their cut from illicit ivory trading; (2) the shadowy and hard to trace network of traders and middlemen who equip the poachers and export the ivory; (3) the buyers in the Gulf States and the Far East who carve the ivory and sell it at immense profits; (4) the poacher himself who gets the least from the whole deal but probably earns an ordinary African's annual wage from the tusks of one elephant. It is a formidable combination to smash, almost as difficult as dealing with the drug trade, the basic difference being that here we are dealing in animal rather than human misery, though aesthetically, human life will be a good deal poorer if the elephant ever becomes extinct. The components of both trades are, however, very similar.

There are two obvious points of attack. The first is to smash the poachers. This requires the will to do so and the money to equip and train the men in the field. The second approach, to place an international ban on trading in ivory, is far more difficult and its effect more questionable.

Kenya has already gone a long way towards winning the first battle.

In early 1989 President Moi appointed Richard Leakey as the Head of Kenya's Wildlife Department. (The Leakeys are a remarkable clan and none more so than Richard. His father and mother, Louis and Mary Leakey, made the great fossil discoveries in Olduvai Gorge which suggested that early man evolved in Africa. Richard subsequently made finds that predated those of his parents. Until his wildlife appointment, Richard was Director of the National Museums of Kenya.) In a typically forceful way, Richard Leakey overhauled his new department from top to bottom. He put new spirit into his ranger forces and equipped them with automatic weapons to match those used by the poachers. For the world at large, and the African ivory trade in particular, Leakey made a spectacular gesture – a mound of £1 million worth of ivory, much of it retrieved from poachers. This was then set alight by President Moi of Kenya. In the first eight months of Dr Richard Leakey's office, over 50 poachers were shot and killed at the cost of one death in his own force of 300 men. In a *Sunday Express* interview Leakey explained his shoot-to-kill policy.

There is probably unnecessary enthusiasm among my men for shooting poachers, but you must realise that we are not shooting unarmed men. These gangs are capable of putting up very effective fire even against our spotter planes ... You have to remember that there is not the same regard for human life in Africa. I know there is some concern that human rights are being violated but we are at war and it can get very violent.

Leakey and many others believe in an international ban on ivory trading. Most of the nations of southern Africa, however, do not. South Africa, Zimbabwe, Botswana all have stable or even increasing elephant populations which are controlled by culling or hunting on licence. These countries claim, with some justification, that the harvesting and selling of ivory is tightly regulated and that the money it produces is ploughed back into conservation. Some of it is channelled through to local people, thus giving them a vested interest in the conservation of elephants.

The body that controls the sale of ivory, among other by-products obtained from rare animals and indeed, rare animals themselves, is called CITES (The Convention on International Trade in Endangered Species); 103 nations are signatories to the Convention which meets at intervals in Switzerland. To impose an international ban on the sale of ivory it would have to place elephants on Appendix One. This it failed to do at its meeting in October 1989.

As I have shown there are two powerful arguments, one for the ban, the other equally strongly against it. There are also those on both sides who are unsure, to say the very least, as to whether the ban would work. Perhaps the strongest argument of the 'ban ivory' enthusiasts led by such authorities as Richard Leakey and Iain Douglas-Hamilton, is that even if the southern African nations rigidly controlled the sale of their legitimate ivory, its very presence in the market place would enable 'dirty' ivory to be laundered.

The battle will rage on for a long time yet, at least as long as there are elephants left to argue over. Is the future really as bleak for the African elephant as is currently thought? If you are talking of large numbers of elephants spread widely across Africa from the west to the east, from the Sudan to the Cape, then the answer has to be yes. What seems most likely is that small populations will continue for a long time in the states that have the will, energy and funds to crush the poacher in the field and thus starve the middleman of raw material.

★

What is happening worldwide to the elephant is happening even faster to another great mammal, the rhinoceros. There are five rhino species, two in Africa and three in the Far East, and all five are on the brink of extinction. They are being killed for the same reason as the elephant – human greed. Both have something out of which man can make a good profit. Elephants are slaughtered for their teeth. Rhinos are killed for the horn on the end of their noses. In the cases of the two African species there are two horns. The three Asian rhinos wear only one. The horn, which is only compacted hair, or at least is made of the same substance as hair, is used for magical and medicinal purposes in many parts of the East. These powers are not only, as is often supposed, of an aphrodisiac nature. In Japan, for example, rhino horn is incorporated in medicines that are said to cure measles, influenza, nose-bleeds and various fevers. In Korea the horn is one of thirty ingredients in a medicine known as Chung Sim Hwan balls used to treat a wide variety of ailments. The aphrodisiac qualities of horn are largely believed in by ageing Indian gentlemen.

For a long time the North Yemen market presented the rhino with one of its gravest threats. In the late 1970s and early 1980s the North Yemen became the biggest single market for African rhino horn. There it was worked into the handles of ornamental daggers. Fortunately, this market tapered off. Almost everyone who could afford these costly ceremonial daggers soon had one. Also the increased use of Western dress made the wearing of such weapons no longer *de rigeur*.

Despite a total ban on rhino horn and skin by CITES in 1976, illicit traders still find plenty of ways round the ban and there are always poachers ready to do the killing. As recently as 1985, four countries still allowed rhino horn across their borders – Taiwan, Macao, Hong Kong and Singapore. One by one, international pressure was applied to them until they fell into line, at least officially. This did not mean that the illicit trade ceased. The first country to react favourably was Taiwan (Republic of China). In August 1985 it announced that exports and imports would be banned forthwith. This did nothing to kill the demand by the consumer. Rhino-horn medicines were still offered in the shops. The retail price for African horn remained at US $1,532 per kilogram and Asian horn (reckoned to be far more effective) stood at US $23,929. Today, with fewer rhinos left in the wild, you can reckon the latter figure in pounds. Though the situation of the African black rhino is bad enough, the pressure put on the three Asian species by these prices is devastating, especially since two of them, the Sumatran and Javan rhinos, are clinging on by the tips of their horns anyway. There may be 500 of the former species left and probably no more than 50 Javan rhinos, all, save maybe 15 recently found in Vietnam, in the Ujong Kulong peninsular close to Krakatoa. Taiwan has become the greatest single market place for rhino horn. Much of this is said to be smuggled in from South Africa, certainly not with official approval though the authorities must know what is going on, if only because South Africa is busily attracting investors from Taiwan. There are over 120 factories financed by Taiwan and 2,000 Taiwanese residents in the country. With regular flights between Johannesburg and Taipei it is not hard to arrange illegal shipments of horn.

Can the world's rhinos be saved from extinction? My own view is that in the wild their future is limited. Despite their unpredictable temperament, they are easy animals to poach. So long as the demand for their quite useless nasal protruberance continues (whoever heard of a patient curing 'flu by drinking chopped up hair in water?), they will go on being slaughtered. The white rhino, increasing in numbers and heavily protected by an efficient national parks system, has the best chance. There are now probably more white rhino in Africa than black. Even twenty years ago nobody would have believed this possible. In 1970 there were an estimated 65,000 black rhinos in Africa and only 3,500 white.

Within India's Kaziranga National Park and Nepal's Royal Chitawan National Park, the great Indian one-horned rhino is probably safe. Though there are very few Sumatran rhino, the smallest of all the species, left in the wild, it is a secretive animal, hard to track down, in the thick forests in which it lives. A scientist friend Marcus Borner, spent several years successfully working on this animal for his PhD thesis but only actually saw one for a few minutes. His work depended largely on deductions and observations made from droppings, chewed food plants and tracks. The Javan rhino is definitely on borrowed time. No population of large mammals that has sunk to just over 50 can have any real species expectation.

This leaves what it probably the most famous of them all, Africa's black rhino. It is known through the tales of explorers and big game hunters and latterly through television wildlife films. It is an explosive, violent and unpredictable beast but extremely easy to find and shoot. Figures produced by the African Elephant and Rhino Specialist Group put the estimated African total at 3,773 in 1978. Zimbabwe, with a policy to shoot poachers without asking questions tops the league with 1,760. South Africa comes next with 580, Kenya (pre-Leakey) is estimated at 520. Sudan, Somalia, Angola, Mozambique and Ethiopia have already almost certainly shot the lot, though nobody knows for sure. Uganda has no rhinos left. In the wild, black rhinos don't have much chance. The rhino expert Dr Bradley Martin, to whom I am indebted for most of these statistics, believes that protecting rhinos inside fenced sanctuaries, like the one recently created at Lake Nakuru by the organisation known as Rhino Rescue, is the only real chance they have got. The Nakuru sanctuary costs £75,000 a year to maintain and patrol and it protects around 20 rhinos.

Twenty-eight years ago, after my own experiences with the rhino catchers in Uganda, I wrote a novel called *The Animal-Catchers* at the end of which, when the catchers released their hard-won rhinos in a country threatened with civil war, the head of the outfit took a hacksaw and cut off his captives' horns. Hornless, he reckoned, they had a chance of surviving for there was no longer a reason for the poachers to kill them. I claim no great credit for what was, after all, only an idea in a work of fiction but recently I saw that wildlife authorities in Namibia, a country that still has some 470 black rhino, were taking a hacksaw to the front end of some of their rhinos. Maybe the only future for those rhino that are left is for them to walk around with nothing on the end of their noses, although the horn would have to be trimmed from time to time. Horn, like the hair it really is, grows again.

9

Put Them Back Alive

National parks offer the only hope of protection now for endangered species like the elephant and rhino. The chances of successfully introducing them back into the wild are too slim to be seriously considered. The outlook, however, is not so bleak for smaller animals and birds. The idea of taking the last survivors of an endangered bird species from its native habitat, breeding them in captivity until they are sufficiently numerous again, and then reintroducing them into the wilderness is an exciting one.

When you consider the rate of extinction, you can understand why conservationists make the attempt at reintroduction, however heavily the odds are stacked against them. In the last 300 years, 163 bird species have become extinct, 76 of them in this century. International bird organisations believe that we shall lose another 40 by the end of the century and that at least 1,000 more are under threat.

The concept of reintroduction is simple enough; the reality is not, as the classic story of the ne-ne, or Hawaiian goose, demonstrates. The ne-ne programme contains most of the problems that beset any attempt to reintroduce a wild animal, bird, mammal, fish, reptile or insect.

The ne-ne is the largest of Hawaii's native land birds. It stands about 1 foot 8 inches high and weighs some 4½ pounds. Its closest relatives are the Lesser Canada, red-breasted, barnacle and black brant-goose. In the mid-eighteenth century there were probably as many as 25,000 ne-nes living at altitudes up to 9,000 feet on Hawaii. In 150 years its numbers were reduced to fewer than 50. In 1949 it was estimated that there were just 35 birds left in the wild. The reasons for this dramatic decline were all familiar ones. Like many island creatures, the goose was remarkably tame and therefore an easy prey to the increasing number of firearms. It was exposed to a four-and-a-half-month hunting season with a bag limit of six birds. At home, Europeans and

Americans shot game during the winter and saw no reason to modify the habit just because they were in mid-Pacific. Unfortunately, their winter and autumn coincided with the birds' nesting season. On top of this, the crews of whaling ships provisioned their vessels with ne-ne meat. Thousands of geese were killed and salted down to victual whale-catchers. Then, the spread of sugar plantations in the lowlands, together with the introduction of sheep and goats, left only the high ground more or less untouched. There, however, introduced predators such as rats and feral pigs and, most of all mongooses, brought in to control the rats, disturbed nesting pairs, ate eggs and killed young.

In the late 1930s Peter Scott, who later founded the Wildfowl Trust, became aware that the ne-ne was in danger of extinction. Scott was then maintaining a small private wildfowl collection at the Old Lighthouse by the mouth of the river Nene at Sutton Bridge, Lincolnshire (the name was a happy coincidence, though river and geese are pronounced quite differently). To add to his collection, Scott asked Herbert Shipman (an Hawaiian ranch owner), for a pair of ne-ne from the flock that he had maintained since 1918 when he first realised the species' existence was threatened. The Second World War intervened, though, and Scott was unable to collect the geese. It was not until the end of the war that two rearing programmes were put into action. In 1949 the Hawaiian Board of Agriculture and Forestry began breeding with two pairs of geese. In 1952 the Wildfowl Trust produced nine goslings from two females and one male. The parents from each project had come from Herbert Shipman's collection.

The overall results, however, were at first disappointing. Poor incubation techniques were partly to blame. The main problem, however, was that although the females produced large clutches, a number of their eggs were infertile. Because these ne-ne all stemmed from Herbert Shipman's collection, it was likely that inbreeding was causing the damage.* An injection of wild stock was badly needed. In 1960, a pair of ne-ne and one young bird were captured and taken to the restoration project headquarters at Pohakuloa on Hawaii. The pair's

---

* At the Wildfowl Trust, Slimbridge, great improvements have been made in feeding, selective breeding and incubation. One brilliant young research worker even perfected an electronic egg. When placed under a sitting hen, the sensors it contained could record temperature at six points of the shell, humidity and the degree of light, which showed whether the female was sitting or standing. All this information could be transmitted to a recorder up to 1 kilometre away. Sadly for ornithological research, the young electronic wizard concerned was snapped up by industry.

offspring were later bred with captive geese both in Hawaii and England with considerable improvement in fertility levels.

By 1966 there were 195 ne-ne at Slimbridge and 124 elsewhere. Between 1952 and 1973, 754 birds, all told, were fledged in England. In March 1960, 20 Hawaiian-reared geese were released to augment the 50 or so birds thought to be still in the wild on Hawaii. Two years later, 30 English-bred ne-ne were put back into the wild, not on Hawaii but on the neighbouring island of Maui. The release area was the 20-square-mile Haleakala Crater where the species had died out during the nineteenth century. All possible precautions were taken in both cases to try to ensure that the birds settled down and did not wander. The releases continued. By June 1978, 1,761 birds had been put down on Maui and Hawaii, the latter being chosen for 1,272 of these.

This was by no means all. It was decided that because the breeding programme in Hawaii was more than able to supply birds for release into the wild, the Wildfowl Trust could sell or give their surplus birds to any zoo or reputable waterfowl collector who wanted them. By 1973, 754 ne-ne were known to have fledged in captive breeding programmes in Europe. There were 232 at Slimbridge alone and at least 200 on loan to other establishments in the UK with 10 more in the USA and 9 in Europe. At this point there were more ne-ne in zoos and collections than in the wild. In this respect the operation was a great success. At least the Hawaiian goose now seemed to have an assured future in captivity. The main objective, however, had been to re-establish the bird in its native habitat. This had not been achieved. Despite numbers injected, despite the healthy captive breeding programmes, despite the effort and devotion of all concerned, the ne-ne in the wild is still, at the moment of writing, clinging on by the tips of its primaries though there are at last signs that a breakthrough may be in sight.

Was it, then, even worth doing? The answer has to be yes. A rare and beautiful bird has been saved from extinction. There is also the tremendous propaganda appeal of a reintroduction programme featuring such an attractive creature. In the case of the ne-ne most bird-lovers, as opposed to knowledgeable ornithologists, have got so used to seeing this handsome goose happily strutting about in wildfowl collections that they can be forgiven for assuming that the effort has been an entire success. It may still be.

The battle, though, is not over, let alone lost. In 1989, the Wildfowl and Wetland Trust put scientists into the field in an attempt to discover what had gone wrong with the release programme and why so few birds had failed to produce young. Follow-up research is as vital to a reintroduction programme as the work that initiates it. Experience shows that the projects are almost always, perhaps inevitably, started too late, when the animal population concerned has already been run down too far. It is argued that you should start planning for reintroduction when the species is still present in large numbers, though likely to dwindle to a critical level in the near future. There would then be a sufficiently varied gene pool on which to base the captive breeding programme. In the case of the ne-ne, the inadequacy of the gene selection showed up in at least two ways. The first was the high rate of infertility. The second was that a high proportion of the chicks bred in captivity matured with soft, fluffy breast feathers, leaving them poorly insulated for the high altitudes at which they were released. This was almost certainly the product of a recessive gene, for recent ne-ne fossil finds suggest that the goose was originally a lowland bird which must have been driven to the high lava slopes by agricultural development and introduced predators.

This, of course, argues that much more research needs to be done on the ground before reintroduction is considered. Time, however, is of the essence and such is the usual run-down rate of an endangered species that the decision on reintroduction has to be taken immediately. As the late Peter Scott pointed out, ideally any such programme should be run in the country concerned rather than divided between several locations. Then there needs to be whole-hearted co-operation between the wildlife experts and the authorities on the spot, something which is seldom achieved. It should be basic to any reintroduction programme that the real causes of the animal's decline be researched and fully understood before any other steps, including captive breeding, are taken. What is more, those destructive factors must be eradicated before time and money are spent in sending in reinforcements.

Despite the partial failure of the ne-ne programme, some bird reintroductions have 'taken' remarkably well. One of the most successful has been the return of the white-tailed sea eagle to the British Isles. This magnificent raptor with a wing-spread of 8 feet had been absent from Britain as a breeding species for 70 years. The last recorded nest was robbed by an egg-collector in 1910. The reintroduction project, run jointly by the Nature Conservancy Council and the Royal Society for the Protection of Birds, began in 1975. Over the next ten years, 82 sea eagles were air-lifted by the RAF from Norway, where they are still common, and reared under the direction of John Love at the National Nature Reserve on the Hebridean island of Rhum. Love later wrote an excellent book about the project.

After initial difficulties, a number of eaglets were reared and released not only on Rhum but elsewhere throughout the Highlands. The reason for the disappearance of the eagle earlier in the century appears to have been straightforward persecution – poisoning and shooting by farmers and fishermen, and nest-robbing by egg-collectors. Sea Eagle nests are usually far more accessible than those of the golden eagle. The attitude of farmers, game-keepers and sportsmen towards birds of prey has, however, improved, although there are undoubtedly exceptions.* One of the reasons why the sea eagle has been able to return to Britain is that, with the co-operation of keepers and land-owners, the nests have been well guarded. The other key to success is that the coastal habitat and the food supply were more or less unchanged and intact, though there is always the risk of oil spills.

At the other extreme is the sad case of the barn owl. The wild population of barn owls in Britain is probably no higher than 7,000 (1989). It is likely to decrease further due to habitat destruction, including hedgerows which provide homes for prey such as fieldmice and voles. The prey animals themselves are increasingly controlled by rodenticides. Lastly, the barn owl's low-level hunting flight at dusk renders it an easy if unintended target for the speeding motor car.

The barn owl is an emotive creature. Its graceful crepuscular flights low over meadow and marsh seem to many to stand for a green Britain that is fast vanishing. All owls are fairly easy to breed in captivity. Not unnaturally a number of private enthusiasts and wildlife trusts rear barn owls and release them into the countryside to, as they see it, bolster up the declining wild population. As many as 2,500 barn owls are thought to be released in this way every year. Unfortunately, very few hand-reared owls are able to fend for themselves when freed. In fact, most are likely to die. The RSPB, which can be expected to be behind any worthwhile move to protect birds, has totally disowned barn owl reintroduction. There are even those who would like to prosecute anyone who releases tame-reared barn owls under the Abandonment of Animals Act, 1960. In contrast to the sea eagle campaign, the barn owl reintroduction is sentimental rather than practical. Though undoubtedly well-meant, almost everything about it is wrong-headed.

One of the most remarkable successes of bird introduction took place in 1970. It concerned two migratory species of European wildfowl, the bean goose and the lesser white-fronted goose. Though it wasn't quite clear why their numbers were decreasing, it seemed probable that

---

* One such occurred in 1989 when a golden eagle died of a shotgun wound on Tayside. A foreign party of grouse shooters were suspected. Courts can impose fines of up to £2,000 for illegal hunting.

habitat changes, increased hunting and disturbance on their southern wintering grounds were the most likely causes. The birds appeared to be perfectly secure on their northern breeding grounds. So it was suggested that it might be possible to 're-route' them onto a safe, or anyway safer, migration flight path. Migratory birds, however, are extremely traditional about the flyways they use and none more so than ducks and geese. The key to success – if it could be achieved – lay in the fact that each new generation learns the migration routes from the adult birds. In 1973, with the support of the World Wildlife Fund, the Swedish scientist Von Essen obtained bean geese eggs from captive birds and then hatched them under feral Canada geese at Oster-Malma, 90 kilometres south-west of Stockholm. When the foster parent Canadas were in moult and their foster chicks still at the downy stage, the families were moved to the bean goose breeding grounds about 350 kilometres to the north-west. There the bean goslings learned to fly and, when autumn came, were led by their foster parents to wintering grounds south of the Baltic. Next spring, when the Canadas returned to Oster-Malma, the bean geese flew on, returning to the nesting grounds where they had learned to fly. These birds and their descendants are now breeding in the reintroduction area and have taught their own progeny the 'safe' migration route they learned from their foster-parents.

So successful was this experiment that it was repeated in 1980 with the lesser white-fronts. This time the 'teachers' were a free-flying family of barnacle geese. The lesser white-fronts given to the barnacles as foster-chicks are now breeding in their traditional breeding grounds but migrating in winter to safer areas used by the barnacle geese.

It is sometimes tempting to reintroduce an endangered species into an entirely new, though suitable, habitat. In the past introductions, rather than reintroductions, have shown how dangerous this can be. The grey squirrel, introduced from North America, did very well in Britain at the expense of the native red squirrel. The British colonists took the mallard, along with many other birds that helped them to feel at home, to New Zealand. Wildfowl are much given to cross-specific marriages. The mallard took a fancy to the native grey duck which it has since swamped with hybridisation. Again, there are several races of Canada geese in North America. As the result of introductions of the wrong sub-species, sometimes by sportsmen, the Canada goose is now a fair mixture of races. This may appear to matter to no one but the taxonomist and the super-purist. Sub-species, however, do not spend many thousands of years evolving their special characteristics for no reason at all but because they equip them better for survival in local conditions. Mix the races up by introductions and the birds that result may well not have these small, although important, adaptations.

On rare occasions it is not the reintroduction of the bird itself that is the main objective. In 1967 the World Wildlife Fund set up Project 406 to collect, breed and study in captivity the white-winged wood duck, one of the world's rarest species of wildfowl. Maintained as a sanctuary was an area of unspoilt primary plains rain forest in Assam where the birds would be reintroduced. The duck's return to its natural habitat had not been, however, the Trust's primary concern, as Michael Ounsted, Head of Developments at the Trust, explains:

The exhibition of white-winged wood duck and successfully breeding them in captivity has enabled us to involve the consumer-oriented children who visit the Trust in great numbers each year in rain forest concern. The first aim of the white-winged wood duck project is to encourage the conservation of primary plains rain forest. The white-winged wood duck is the tangible catalyst that could achieve this. Only when visitors see a victim of rain forest destruction at Slimbridge does the bell ring.

Reintroduction is not, of course, confined to birds. In the 1960s the large blue butterfly became extinct in Britain. Its last habitat was on the cliff tops of Cornwall, near Bude. Theoretically, this butterfly should be one of the hardest to reintroduce. Not only is it reliant on one particular food plant, wild thyme, but it has a most complicated life-cycle. At a crucial stage in the caterpillar's development it has to be taken underground and nursed, almost caressed, by ants if it is to reach the pupal stage.

Like many British rarities, including birds such as the avocet, the black-tailed godwit, the ruffe, and the osprey, the large blue is fairly common on the continent of Europe and in Scandinavia. In 1983, adults and eggs were brought in from Sweden. Suitable colony sites were found in South Devon that were not only secure from the general public but contained both a food supply of wild thyme and the all-important red ant colonies. Rabbit grazing was increased on the sites, so encouraging a shorter sward and favouring the growth of wild thyme and the development of red ant colonies. As a result, 4,500 eggs and 150 adults were recorded in 1989, the large blue's numbers doubling in one year.

*

If the ne-ne is the most publicised bird reintroduction, the starring role among mammals is, without doubt, played by the Arabian oryx. In

1960 the world population of this large desert antelope was reckoned to be down to between 100 and 200 animals. In 1961 a raiding party from Qatar entered the Aden Protectorate in motor vehicles and shot every oryx they could find. The Fauna Preservation Society of London, funded by WWF and the *Daily Mail* and led by Major Ian Grimwood, the Chief Game Warden of Kenya, immediately contacted the Survival Commission of IUCN and together they launched Operation Oryx.

There was never any doubt about the cause of the decline. The oryx was hunted in vehicles by local sheiks and gunned down; once sighted in the empty spaces of the desert, it had virtually no chance of escape. Even while the expedition was being formed and equipped, the news came that the Qataris had returned and, as one message that reached Grimwood put it, 'had shot the lot'. In late April 1962, the expedition set out from Aden (now in South Yemen) in the hope that reports had been exaggerated. At first all they found were the tracks of the raiding Qataris, but on 5 May they caught their first oryx. In the next three weeks only three more were captured. Of these a male died from old gunshot wounds and the stress of capture. This left a non-viable breeding unit of two males and one female. Where to send captured oryx had always been a problem. There were no suitable reserves or national parks in the area where the captives could be safely released. In the end, and with some reluctance, it was agreed to send them to the newly-formed Maytag Zoo in Phoenix, Arizona. The climate there is similar to that the animals had been used to in Arabia. In October 1963, the female gave birth to a calf and the world herd of Arabian oryx came into existence. By 1972 the herd numbered 34 animals. To avoid epidemic diseases, the animals were then split up between various zoos. San Diego, Los Angeles, London, Texas, East Berlin, Hamburg, Rotterdam and Zurich all played their parts. By 1979 the stud book recorded 159 males and 163 females, 48 calves having been born during the year – the keeping of stud books is vital to captive breeding of mammals so that inbreeding and the subsequent appearance of recessive genes can be avoided.*

The original aim of Operation Oryx had been to reintroduce the antelope to the wild. The obvious place had seemed to be Jordan with two national parks at Azraq and Wadi Rum. Both these reserves, however, turned out to be too close to the Saudi Arabian border and the

---

* The exception that seems to break all rules where inbreeding is concerned is the golden hamster. Every golden hamster ever bred stems from the discovery of one pregnant female in a cave in Syria – by pure chance she must have been free of any harmful genes.

risk of further motorised hunting too great. At the intermediary stage only four males and four females were sent to a 22-kilometre fenced reserve at Azraq. The hoped-for reintroduction was finally made in Oman after Sultan Qaboos bin Said and his government had decreed that the oryx was to be given total protection. The area chosen for the release was the Jiddat al Harasis where the last wild oryx had been seen. The Harasis, the local people, were keen to see the oryx back and were ready to guard them. San Diego Zoo sent 14 animals and within the year, 1981, a calf was born in the pens. In January 1982 the scientists in charge declared that the oryx had built up a stable social structure* while in the holding pens and were ready for release. Five of the herd were fitted with radio collars so that their movements could be monitored after release. On 31 January 1982, the gates were opened and the animals allowed to move freely back into their native desert only ten years after the last wild Arabian oryx was thought to have been killed. The last chapter in the oryx story has not yet been written but Operation Oryx seems to have succeeded on two fronts, reintroduction into the original habitat and perpetuation of the species in the shape of a captive world herd.

*

The ethics and value of reintroductions will be argued over for some time to come. The further one goes into the reintroduction jungle, the more tangled the undergrowth of opinion and even prejudice becomes. Hans Meltofte of the Zoological Museum of Copenhagen puts it like this: 'In my opinion the element of originality in nature is reduced every time we manage in one way or another ... Manipulations of populations and individuals should be limited to species which are at total risk of extinction.' Possibly the last word should go to Dr Janet Kear who writes in the final paragraph of her book *The Hawaiian Goose*: 'Only as a last resort, as with the ne-ne, should animals be taken into captivity, bred and released.'

---

* The importance of releasing well-bonded herds has been demonstrated in other mammal reintroductions. The golden tamarin, a tiny South American monkey, is now confined to a small area of rain forest between the coastal mountains and the Atlantic in the State of Rio de Janeiro in Brazil. Several releases were made but it was only when family groups with well-established internal bonds were reintroduced that any success was achieved. Similar techniques have been used by Jersey Zoo where Gerald Durrell has done such fine work with endangered species. When reintroducing the hutia, a small aquatic rodent of the coypu family, to Jamaica, the animals were reared in captivity in groups of up to 18 members.

10

Islands in a Time Warp

Reintroduction, indeed every act of wildlife conservation, only has a chance of succeeding where the original habitat is largely intact and undamaged, isolated from any harmful influences. There are few such places left. Even at the North and South Poles, man's harmful influence is felt in terms of pollution and radiation. The islands of the Galapagos, in the Pacific 600 miles out from the coast of Ecuador, are not only a suitable case for the isolation treatment, they are arguably the international conservation movement's most important patient. Both Ecuador, the country which owns the archipelago, and international conservation organisations are making every effort not only to cure the islands of the ailments man has already brought to them, but also to quarantine them from further infection.

There are a number of urgent reasons why the 13 main islands and 43 islets that make up the Galapagos archipelago should be singled out for this special treatment, one being that many of their life forms are unique to the islands. It was in the Galapagos, during a five-week visit in His Majesty's survey ship *Beagle* in 1835, that Charles Darwin made many of the observations that were to play a leading part in his theories on evolution. The Galapagos are often referred to as 'a living laboratory of evolution'. Obviously this can only remain true if the evolution of the unique species and sub-species is allowed to continue, as far as possible, in isolation, unhindered by man's interference and especially the introduction, deliberately or accidentally, of non-indigenous flora and fauna. Darwin only had time and opportunity to record some of the wildlife wonders of the islands. Nevertheless the animals on which he concentrated were, in an evolutionary sense, the key ones – in particular the 13 species of finches, sometimes known as Darwin's finches.

Darwin concluded that these 13 species had all evolved from one ancestral finch which is believed to have been a small mainland bird called the black-blue grass-quit. Darwin postulated that the original finches had reached the islands some hundreds of thousands of years earlier and that their descendants had become modified when adapting to local conditions and especially the available food niches. They had evolved through the process of natural selection, or to put it in popular terms, survival of the fittest. Not only were new species formed, but new sub-species evolved to make the most of conditions on different islands. In this they were helped by the fact that strong winds and powerful currents prevented much interchange between the islands, leaving each population free to evolve in its own slightly different way and thus become a sub-species. This sub-specification applied not only to the finches but to several other Galapagos creatures including the mocking birds and giant tortoises.

Darwin was prompted to study the tortoises after the Governor pointed out that the carapaces, or shells, of these enormous reptiles varied in shape from island to island. The tortoises on Hood, or Espanola, Island (most islands in the archipelago have British as well as Spanish names) had shells that were highly arched in front to allow the animal to reach up to the prickly pear plants. Those who lived in the lush uplands of Santa Cruz had a flattened, domed carapace – they grazed at ground level and therefore did not need great neck movement. The tortoises, too, had a common mainland ancestor – like the finches they had evolved differently after arrival. It is highly probable that the tortoises made the 600-mile ocean journey from mainland South or central America on rafts of floating vegetation.

Holding as it does, so many unique life forms, it is little wonder that scientists would like to wrap the archipelago in a time warp, keeping it as close as possible to the way the original animal colonists found it. Alas, this is no longer possible. It was not even possible when Darwin reached the islands' shores. Change began almost from the moment the first man set eyes on the Galapagos.

*

That first man was the Bishop of Panama together with the crew of his small ship. In 1538, Fray Tomas de Berlanga was caught in a calm on a voyage from Panama to Peru. Ocean currents carried him 500 miles off course to a group of hitherto unknown islands. On his return he wrote a fascinating account to his Emperor, Charles V of Spain, describing the great black lizards that thronged the lava shoreline. He commented on the tameness of every creature he encountered. The one thing he didn't do was to give his discovery a name. That was left to the Spanish navigators that followed. The same currents that had carried the bishop off course made the islands extremely hard to find. For this reason the early sailors called then *Los Encantadas*, the enchanted islands. The other name given to them has stuck, *Los Galapagos*, after the giant tortoises that the sailors found there.

The onslaught on the islands, or at least on their fauna, didn't start until the late seventeenth century. Pirates and buccaneers who raided the Spanish mainland cities and the ports of Central and South America found the Galapagos an ideal haven. They were far enough away from avenging Spanish ships to be safe; they could refit and careen their ships on the few sheltered beaches; and the islands also offered an abundant supply of food. What was even better, it was food that would keep fresh below decks for up to a year. All you had to do with a giant Galapagos tortoise was to feed it from time to time and it would eventually feed you. Compared with what was to come, the pirates did comparatively little damage to the tortoise population, although they did bring a curse to the islands from which the wildlife has never recovered. When they hauled their ships out for a refit, the black rat took shore leave and found the islands very much to its liking. The wildlife of the Galapagos had previously not had to deal with an efficient mammal predator. The black rat is, unfortunately, one of the best in the business. Far worse was still to come.

Between 1780 and 1860, British and American whalers and sealers invaded the islands. The sperm whale had already been almost hunted out in the North Atlantic but large numbers of these great cetaceans could still be found around the most westerly islands of the Galapagos. In addition, fur seals were still abundant everywhere. In 80 years the whalers and sealers took away an estimated 1,000 giant tortoises to supply them with fresh meat and oil during their long voyages. Unfortunately, many of these were females as they were smaller and easier to stow in the holds. The seamen not only hunted the sperm whale to the point at which it was no longer worth cruising in the islands' waters but they nearly exterminated the Galapagos fur seal, another unique sub-species, killed in tens of thousands for their skins. One sealer, Captain Benjamin Morrel, boasted that he killed 5,000 fur seals in two months. By the 1930s the fur seal was practically wiped out.

Settlers came after the hunters, admittedly in limited numbers, but they brought with them goats, dogs and cats that escaped and went wild, and there are few hunting animals more devastating to small wildlife than a feral cat. It is hard to say which were worst for the native flora and fauna, the cats or the goats. Cats ate young seabirds and iguanas but the goats ate everything. Once established, both goats and cats are desperately hard to eradicate on the rough lava terrain of which most of the islands consist.

At present only about 10,000 Ecuadorian settlers live on the islands and only four of the 13 main islands are occupied, but the population rate is growing by about 4 per cent each year and is bound to increase. The Galapagos are as much part of Ecuador as the mainland and any citizen of the country is free to settle there. Can the islands therefore be kept, as it were, in quarantine so that their unique flora and fauna are not further damaged by unwanted introductions? The answer is almost certainly no but that won't stop the scientists trying.

The first step towards protecting the islands came in 1959 when Ecuador made the Galapagos a national park. Then, in 1964, the Charles Darwin Foundation opened a research station at Academy Bay on the island of Santa Cruz. Up to that point little if any in-depth study of such strange creatures as marine iguanas, the world's only sea-going lizards, giant tortoises and flightless cormorants had been attempted. The Charles Darwin Research Station had an even more urgent task for the immediate future. By 1968 the Ecuadorian Parks Service had been formed. The Charles Darwin Station had to train wardens and guides quickly. Ecuador is not a rich nation and has a great need to earn foreign currency by attracting tourists to the Galapagos. The scientists might not care much for the idea, but the living museum would have to open its doors to the general public and therein lay obvious dangers. Might not the blue-footed boobies, the waved albatrosses, the flightless cormorants, the Galapagos penguins and all the rest of the almost absurdly tame wild creatures start to develop a terror of man? They had never been persecuted by man before and had few natural predators. It's a sad reflection on mankind that almost the only Galapagos animal to show a slight fear of the human shape is the fur seal.

Inflexible rules for visitors were drawn up. Only certain islands could be visited and then only certain parts of those islands. Trails were marked out among the birds and iguanas to which visitor parties, limited to 30 people, had to rigidly comply. From the point of view of the visitor who had paid to watch Galapagos wildlife, this turned out to be no disadvantage. Albatrosses built their nests right next to the trails and sometimes on them. Only one cruise ship at a time was allowed to call at any visitor site; each party had to have a trained guide in charge, and all the guides went through a three-month course in order to obtain their three-year licence, at the end of which they had to take a further examination in order to have it renewed.

By the late 1980s, over 20,000 visitors, mostly Ecuadorians, were visiting the islands under these rules without any apparent damage being caused. If there was a criticism it was that more of the tourist-generated revenue should have been routed directly to the National Park and the Darwin Station.

Will the human invasion remain under control? No-one can be sure about that. There is always talk of building larger cruise ships. There has been talk, too, about opening up a big resort hotel, a proposal that was quashed largely as the result of international pressure. The temptation to develop the islands is, however, always there.

In many ways the Darwin Research Station is the oceanic counterpart of the Serengeti Research Institute in Tanzania: only top-class young scientists are chosen to work there, dependent on university and other grants. These are seldom enough to provide them with even a short-wave radio, so that they have to rely on hailing a chance tourist charter yacht or the Darwin Station's motor cruiser *Beagle* for help in an emergency. There is often no fresh water on the islands; jerricans of water are dropped off by passing boats, along with other rations. Life for a scientist marooned in the Galapagos is no desert island picnic. The reward, apart from the personal satisfaction of having survived, is possibly a PhD and almost certainly an addition to the world's understanding of the islands' unique flora or fauna.

The scientists' research will add to the store of knowledge needed to protect the islands and their species in the future. But what of the fight to restore some of the damage man has done in the past? This battle to put the clock back, or at least halt it where it stands, is ceaseless. Fortunately there are already victories on some fronts. Here some of the problems are the familiar ones of conservation anywhere. On some islands past depredations have almost exterminated the native fauna. When the Darwin Station arrived in the Galapagos, the Espanola, or Hood, Island tortoise seemed doomed to extinction. There were so few tortoises on Espanola that they probably hadn't bred for fifty years simply because a pair hadn't met to mate. The first search of the island produced four, luckily these included males and females. Later two males and 11 females were rounded up and the San Diego Zoo contributed another male to give genetic variation. The eggs went into incubators and a surprising number were hatched, surprising because zoos had never been very successful at breeding giant tortoises – another argument for carrying out reintroduction programmes in the country of origin. An all-out campaign had to be waged, though, against the tortoise's main competitor, the goat. On Espanola this was relatively easy. The island is only a few miles long and is a flat-topped slab of upthrust lava so there weren't too many places for them to hide.

By 1979 the first young tortoises were ready for release. By 1985, 151 tortoises reared at the station had been released on to a goatless Espanola where there would now be enough vegetation left for them to eat.

A nasty shock was to come, however. Experts had discovered that the sex of a tortoise is governed not by genetics but by the temperature at which its egg is incubated. Tortoises in the wild get round this by burying their eggs at different depths. Because there is no way of determining the sex of a very small tortoise, it was a long time after the release before the scientists knew whether there was a healthy balance of the sexes among the young tortoises. Had all that hard work been for nothing? Had the Espanola re-stocking been a one-sex affair? After a time it would be possible to tell by the shape of the carapace. Luckily, more by good luck than scientific judgment, the early releases did include both sexes.

Reintroduction programmes are still being carried out on the islands of Santiago, Pinzon, Santa Cruz, San Christobel and Isabela. Over 800 tortoises of the various island sub-species have been released. The war against the goats continues. So rugged is the terrain on many of these islands that it is never likely to end let alone end in complete victory.

*

Reintroduction and predator control programmes are also being conducted for land iguanas whose predators are feral dogs and cats, marine turtles whose eggs are dug up by pigs, and the rare dark-rumped or Hawaiian petrel (nearly extinct in Hawaii) whose nesting colonies are beset by rats. The roots of wildlife destruction in the Galapagos lie, as we have seen, in the past. But, there is real concern about what may invade the islands in the future. The more visitors and settlers, the greater the risk of an ecological imbalance. If the fauna doesn't suffer any more, the flora is increasingly likely to become a victim. It is comparatively easy to control the release, intentional or otherwise, of harmful mammals but far from easy to monitor the influx of unwanted insects and seeds.

In 1910 fire ants invaded the islands, probably in a load of imported building timber. Once there, they spread. Fire ants are particularly vicious. On the island of Floreana they invaded a petrel colony and drove the birds off their nests. Once established, fire ants spread at the rate of 150 metres a year. They will attack anything great or small. Recently they reached the island of Santa Fé. A firebreak was built and the whole area incinerated.

It is more difficult to keep out alien plants. Seeds have been brought to the Galapagos – borne on the wind, washed ashore by the waves and transported in the plumage or stuck to the feet of seabirds – ever since volcanic action pushed the islands up from the sea bed three to five million years ago. Though the point is possibly arguable in a strict Darwinian sense, natural means is not taken to mean introduction via the shoes or on the clothing of tourists, settlers, sailors or fishermen, yet it is often impossible to prevent. When a large part of the island of Isabela caught fire as the result of farmers burning diseased coffee bushes, army fire-fighting teams had to be brought in from the mainland. Roads were built on the slopes of the volcano Sierra Negra to get their equipment to the scene of action. Here was an obvious route by which alien seeds could enter on military clothing or equipment and be distributed.

The fire damage was plain to see and will repair itself in time, though the scar made by the roads will take longer to disappear. But what if some non-indigenous plants invaded with the 300 soldiers who fought the fire? Perhaps they didn't. If they did it will take some time to become apparent. What is certain is that more and more opportunities for alien invasion will occur as time goes by. In their efforts to keep the islands in quarantine, the Director of the Darwin Station as well as the Director of the National Park face many dilemmas, some of them slightly comical. For example, there is the sad case of 'Lonesome George'.

George is, as far as is known, the last surviving giant tortoise of the remote Pinta island sub-species. Alas for George and posterity it is too late to put the clock back for his island race; there is no Pinta Island female with whom he can mate. In the past there have been suggestions that he should be allowed to court a female from one of the other islands, preferably one whose tortoises most resemble the nearly vanished Pinta sub-species. The idea has been turned down. George is condemned to possibly another hundred years of celibacy rather than be allowed to sire progeny of a bastard race.

If George posed a problem for the scientists of the Galapagos, consider the case of the Puerto Ayora green iguana. Puerto Ayora on the island of Santa Cruz is the main harbour of the Galapagos. The Darwin Station has its base there at Academy Bay. The green iguana, a large lizard common on the mainland of Central and South America, is judged to be the ancestor of the two unique species of Galapagos iguanas. The theory, and it is a highly probable one, is that millions of years ago, the green iguana or its ancestor got carried to the Galapagos from the mainland, probably on a raft of floating vegetation. It may even have swum part of the way. Possibly the first iguana to make the voyage was a gravid female. Over a vast period of time it is likely that there were other iguana immigrants. Once arrived, they adapted to local conditions. In the process they diverged into two very distinct species, the sea-going and sea-feeding marine iguana, a blue-black, swarthy, blunt-nosed beast with a modified, flattened tail for swimming and the large yellow, cactus-eating land iguana. Scientists can demonstrate that it would only be necessary for one pregnant green iguana to make one successful landfall once every 50,000 years for things to have turned out as they have.

Now for a moment of drama. Recently, the current 50,000-year period seemed to have produced its immigrant. A green mainland iguana was found swimming in the harbour at Puerto Ayora. There was high excitement. Was this the living proof that things had happened just the way everyone had imagined? Then cooler judgments deflated the moment of unscientific euphoria. Puerto Ayora is not only the main harbour, it is also the port of call for the tourist steamers plying from the mainland. Wasn't it more likely that this reptile invader had hitched a ride as a stowaway or had even been released by a visitor or crew member? Had the unfortunate reptile arrived on the shores of a less-visited and more remote island, such as Genovesa to the north or distant and inaccessible Wolf Island, then it would have had a far better chance of being accepted as positive confirmation of long-held theories. Instead, it found itself dead in a bottle of spirit as a laboratory specimen.

Here is another dilemma which is purely hypothetical. The entire world population of Galapagos flightless cormorants lives around the shores of the island of Fernandina and the neighbouring island of Isabela. There are only a few hundred of them all told. Fernandina consists mainly of one huge and very active volcano and the brittle lava floes running down from it. In fact, the Galapagos are one of the most volcanic areas on earth. In 1968 when Fernandina last exploded, the crater lake at its centre fell 2,000 feet. It is therefore easy to imagine a cataclysmic eruption that threatens every flightless cormorant in the world since they are all within lava range of Fernandina. Being flightless, the cormorant has little chance of escaping. It can swim very well above and below the surface but even this ability is unlikely to save it from the shower of ash and streams of lava about to descend on its nesting grounds. The volcano doesn't erupt without warning so that the National Park and the Darwin Station have just enough time to act and, of course, realising what is likely to happen to this unique bird the international conservation bodies are ready to help mount a rescue operation.

But, should the cormorants be rescued? Before all this modern technology and science came on the scene, even 50 years ago, wouldn't the bird have had to take its chances and possibly pay the ultimate price of being flightless? In a Darwinian sense, might it not have been judged by nature as not being quite up to the job? It's possible, but can you see that being allowed to happen in the modern conservation climate? A much more likely scenario, I feel, is one in which Prince Philip arrives in the *Britannia*, having diverted the royal yacht specially, while on a state visit to Panama. The President of Ecuador flies in by private jet to give the operation official blessing and every last flightless cormorant is airlifted to safety by helicopters of the Ecuadorian Air Force. Such a situation makes one wonder where playing God starts or, for that matter, ends.

I I

The Front-line Fighters

To have a chance of saving any wild creature, whether it is the unique flightless cormorant of the Galapagos or the insignificant noisy scrub bird of Western Australia, conservationists must first get the public on their side. Only when enough ordinary men and women all over the world realise the importance of winning the wildlife war can there by any hope of influencing those who have the power to make or break the environment.

Naturally it is far easier to persuade people who have a high standard of living that wildlife and wild places are worth saving. If you are an African subsistence farmer with too many children and a ten-year drought to contend with, the last thing on your mind is likely to be the plight of the black rhino. Fortunately, if hearts and minds – and wallets – can most readily be won in the developed countries, it is those countries who can most afford to support and encourage worldwide conservation. No-one should under-estimate the power of the individual, for it is he or she who puts politicians and hence governments in power and is the customer on whom industry depends. By and large it is government and industry which can do most good or, more frequently, most harm to wildlife. Public pressure is, however, influencing these powerful institutions. An international bank withdraws financial support for an industrial development that would have devastated yet more rain forest. At the consumer end of things, a tin of tuna fish bears the label 'dolphin-friendly'. This means that the fish has been caught by line rather than by net (nets drown thousands of dolphins annually). Neither the future of the bank-threatened rain forest nor the fate of net-drowned dolphins would have been considered if public opinion had not been active in supporting their causes, or if activists had not campaigned vigorously in support of conservation during the crucial three or four decades covered by this book. In saving wildlife, the campaigner has played a role every bit as important as the biologist in the field or the warden with the dart gun.

Effective wildlife campaigners are of two kinds – the dedicated individual and the well-organised, well-led pressure group which should be, but seldom is, well funded. Both kinds have already been seen in action in this book.

Individual campaigners fall into distinct categories though they all have one thing in common – their total dedication to wildlife. In almost every case it is certain that their work would have had little or, anyway, far less impact had television or the film industry not 'discovered' them. The Adamsons were outstanding examples of this. George Adamson was a game warden in the arid Northern Frontier District of Kenya. One morning in February 1956, he was forced to shoot a lioness suspected of being a man-eater. She had three very small cubs which Adamson took back to camp. In time, the two biggest cubs had to be sent away to Rotterdam Zoo but the smallest, called Elsa, remained as part of the Adamson family. The rest is history. Elsa grew up as a close and loving friend. Eventually she learned to hunt for herself and returned to the wild where she bore her own cubs which she brought to visit the Adamsons' camp. Joy Adamsom wrote a book *Born Free* about Elsa's upbringing which became a world bestseller and was followed by the sequel *Living Free*. Highly successful feature films were made of both. Elsa and the Adamsons became powerful symbols of what saving wildlife is all about and probably did as much as the rescue at Kariba had done earlier to awaken public sympathy.

Television has played a key part in campaigning for wildlife – admittedly, as in the case of the cinema, primarily for its own ends. Wildlife programmes are universally popular. They command high audience ratings, are uncontroversial, apolitical and sell all over the world. Television has therefore been able to bring into millions of homes the heroic efforts of some of wildlife's most ardent campaigners whose work would not otherwise have had the same tremendous impact.

One such conservationist was Dian Fossey. She was a children's occupational therapist in Louisville, Kentucky and had always dreamed of going to Africa. Her imagination was especially fired by the work done by George Schaller on the mountain gorillas of Mount Mikeno in the then Belgian Congo. Schaller, a research associate of the New York Zoological Society, had become, through field studies carried out all over the world, the doyen of wildlife ecologists. Fossey also wanted to meet Louis and Mary Leakey at Olduvai Gorge in Tanzania, the site of their historic fossil finds of early man. Dian achieved her first ambition and got Leakey's permission to walk round some recent

Right Jane Goodall, the world's expert on chimpanzees, began her work with little scientific training and no experience of Africa.

Greenpeace activists in head-on confrontation with Russian whalers.

excavations in the Gorge. She slipped and fell into the 'dig', breaking her right ankle and, with the pain, vomited all over the precious fossil being uncovered. Despite this, she obviously made a deep impression on the Leakeys, especially when she told them of her determination to climb the Virunga volcanoes to make contact with the gorillas. Mary Leakey warned her that, after her fall, she would be unwise to climb over 10,000 feet.

A fortnight later the Leakeys heard that Fossey, with her ankle bound up and aided by a stick, her African driver and a dozen porters, had made the five-hour climb to the Kabara meadow which Schaller had used as a base for his field work.

Three years later, Louis Leakey visited her in Louisville where she was back working as an occupational therapist. He suggested that she become his 'gorilla girl' to carry out a long-term study, much as Jane Goodall, whom he had earlier helped to put into the field, was doing with chimpanzees at Gombe Stream in Tanzania. There was one condition; since Dian was likely to be cut off from medical aid for long periods, she must have her appendix removed first. Dian readily agreed. She would, she confessed later, have agreed to anything. Returning from hospital, Dian found a letter from Dr Leakey which said: 'Actually, there isn't any dire need for you to have your appendix removed. It is just my way of testing applicants' determination.'

Shortly after Dian was installed on Mount Mikeno she was caught up in the disturbances in the new state of Zaire which had replaced the Belgian Congo. In July 1967, in peril of her life, she fled to Uganda, certain that she would never see her gorillas again. Then, largely due to the efforts of Louis Leakey, she got a fresh start in neighbouring Rwanda. At 10,000 feet, close to the summit of another of the Virunga volcanoes, Mount Visoke, she set up her Karisoke Research Centre. Here she did most of her important behavioural studies on the mountain gorilla.

Dian Fossey was a quite different sort of campaigner from Joy Adamson. Her approach was more scientific, though, as with the Adamsons and Elsa, she had a personal relationship with 'her' animals. She was passionate in defence of the gorillas, so much so that she frequently made enemies among officials in whose country she was, after all, working as a guest. The two main threats to the mountain gorilla were, and are, poaching and loss of habitat. In fighting against both she was bound to meet strong local opposition.

Dian Fossey's work to save a threatened species might have gone largely unnoticed but for the influence of the media, including television. All private research workers in the wildlife field need a sponsor.

Should that role be fulfilled by the *National Geographic* magazine, they are extremely fortunate. This hugely successful journal with a world-wide reputation and circulation sponsors many of the best environ-mental causes, and certainly some of the best scientists, including Dian Fossey. The *National Geographic* also makes films on wildlife and the environment, one such featuring Dian and her apes.

On a scientific level, the importance of Dian's work is marked by the fact that in 1980 Cornell University made her a Visiting Associate Professor. There is no doubt that if the mountain gorilla survives in any numbers in Rwanda, the campaigning work of Dian Fossey will have been largely responsible.

Her remarkable career ended in tragedy. One night she was killed with a panga in her room at her research centre on Mount Visoke. No-one has ever discovered who was responsible. One theory says that gorilla poachers committed the murder, another that the killing was political, a third that she was slashed to death as an act of reprisal. She certainly made enemies. At one time she kidnapped an African child in retaliation for the killing of one of her gorillas. Her murder may simply have been without motive.* After her death her life and work was portrayed in the feature film *Gorillas in the Mist*. Through this film her campaigning zeal survived even after her death.

Across the border in Zaire, on the slopes of Mounts Kahuzi and Biega, similar campaigning work on behalf of the mountain gorilla was being carried out by a remarkable Belgian called Adrien Deschryver. Unlike Fossey, Deschryver had no scientific aspirations. His family had owned coffee plantations at Kahuzi-Biega. Throughout the civil war in the Congo, he had maintained a spirited, almost single-handed defence of these properties, at one time capturing 300 Simba rebels with a Jeep and a heavy machine-gun. After the war, this soft-spoken, gentle man decided he had seen enough violence and that he would dedicate his life to protecting the mountain gorillas that lived in and

---

* By a sad coincidence, all three of the wildlife campaigners described above were murdered. Joy Adamson was chopped to death by a disgruntled African servant. In 1989 her husband George was killed by Shifta bandits at Kora, his reserve in Northern Kenya, while trying to defend friends. Of these three deaths only one, that of Dian Fossey, was possibly connected with wildlife work. Conservation has produced its martyrs. In 1989 Chico Mendes, the South American who campaigned for the protection of the Brazilian rain forests, was killed by unknown assassins. He had fought against the ranchers who wished to obliterate the forests to run cattle there.

around his plantations. In the 1970s, I had the privilege of working with Adrien Deschryver, making a film of his work with the gorillas that got national network showing on NBC in the United States as well as in Britain. Once again television became the means of bringing an all-important wildlife campaigner's fight for an endangered species to a large audience.

Since films of both Dian Fossey's and Adrien Deschryver's work appeared on worldwide television, a good deal has happened on the Virunga volcanoes, some of which is no doubt due to the publicity given to the gorillas on film and television. Despite some poaching for souvenirs (it is a grisly thought that anyone should actually want a gorilla's foot, hand or head as a keepsake), the total population of gorillas is increasing, with a high percentage of young animals recorded.

The Fauna and Flora Preservation Society, together with the African Wildlife Foundation and the World Wide Fund for Nature, have formed the Mountain Gorilla Project based on Rwanda. This has provided funds for the equipment and training of wardens. As a result there are signs that poaching is being brought under control.

★

None of the wildlife campaigners I have described started from a scientific background though some were later honoured by that world. It is rare to find a 'pure' scientist who is willing to divert, however briefly, from the mainstream of his work to make the considerable effort needed to produce a film about it. In doing so, he or she runs the risk of having the label 'populariser' attached to them which is, in some scientists' eyes, a serious crime. Nevertheless some of the best individual campaigners, as opposed to organised pressure groups, have been scientists first and foremost. Roger Payne, the American expert on whales, can certainly be included among these.

I first met Roger Payne when making a film shot by the Australian wildlife camera team Des and Jen Bartlett – no mean campaigners themselves through their films, writings and stills published in the *National Geographic*. This Survival 'Special', called 'The Passing of Leviathan' was about the southern right whale and was shot on a desolate part of the coast of Patagonia, the Gulf of San Matias, 600 miles south of Buenos Aires, I remember interviewing Roger Payne and taping his replies when we started planning the film. When I asked him why he felt so strongly about whales, he said:

'If you're a small animal you lead a frantic frightened life. But if you're a whale, all but the grandest things must pass beneath your notice. As the largest animal that ever lived, including the dinosaurs, you can afford to be gentle and view life without fear. It's this sense of tranquility, life without urgency, power without aggression, that has completely won my heart to whales.'

Now that may not be a strictly scientific statement it may even have tinges of anthropomorphism about it but it is most certainly passionate. With his wife Katy, Roger did much of the pioneer research into the behaviour not only of right whales but also of the humpback whale. Together they recorded, analysed and came to know a great deal about the meaning of the humpback's mysterious song. They discovered that the whales who returned to the Hawaiian islands to breed each year sang a slightly different song each season, adding or changing phrases. The song was without doubt a means of communication.

This man's love of whales showed in everything he said about them. 'For hours at a time,' he once told me, 'my wife Katy and I sailed in the company of whales listening to their songs. I think there is nothing that has happened to me that can compare with those days. Rocking gently in a boat with those sounds flooding out of the sea is like no other experience.'

He believed that nothing short of a 50-year moratorium on killing could save the great whales from destruction and campaigned for this on film and paper. At one crucial point he played a leading part in persuading the United States government to put a ban on the import of whale products. He has also fought the whales' cause at meetings of the International Whaling Commission, from which Japan, the nation with the worst whaling record in the world, once tried to exclude him. There is a strange footnote to the story of the Paynes as scientific campaigners. In 1970, Roger Payne talked a record company into pressing a long-player of his whale recordings. I readily confess that 'Songs of the Humpback Whale' is not my favourite listening. Nevertheless it became a bestseller and a cult record treasured by collectors. In this way it played a considerable part in the propaganda war to protect the great whales. It is possible that the unearthly sounds it reproduces speak to the listener of life's sea origins and therefore touch the emotions deeply.

★

Impressive as the results obtained by individual campaigners have been – and, of course, I am sadly aware that I have missed out many equally deserving of notice – the importance of the well-organised pressure group cannot be over-emphasised. The enemy forces are numerous and well-led. To combat them, or preferably to convert them, demands a similar degree of organisation, reasoned argument and action. Sometimes it is necessary to declare an outright but non-violent state of war. Greenpeace has an impressive list of battle honours in such wars. Founded in 1971 it claims 2 million members, over 170,000 being in the United Kingdom. Whereas Friends of the Earth concerns itself with broader ecological issues – the greenhouse effect, acid rain, pollution, the excesses of the consumer society and, more importantly, the excesses of industries that nurture the consumer society – Greenpeace acts more directly on situations which mainly concern this book, describing itself as 'an international environmental pressure group which acts against abuse to the natural world'.

It began in 1971 when a group of American and Canadian environmentalists chartered a boat to take them to the Aleutian Islands, where the United States planned a series of nuclear tests. Greenpeace demonstrations generated a great deal of publicity which played a large part in having the tests called off after one explosion.

In 1977, the year the Greenpeace opened a London office, the organisation bought an international campaign ship called the *Sir William Hardy* (renamed *Rainbow Warrior*), a former North Sea trawler and Ministry of Agriculture research ship which had been found derelict in the London docks. Within a year she was harrying Icelandic whale-catchers by launching high speed small boats between them and the rorquals their harpoon gunners were attempting to shoot. The ship's crew made such a nuisance of themselves that Icelandic fishery patrol boats arrested them and confiscated gear, although they were operating in international waters. The *Rainbow Warrior* later carried out campaigns against dumping nuclear waste at sea and the proposed killing of over 3,000 grey seal pups in the Orkneys. She was 'arrested' in La Coruna on the west coast of Spain by the Spanish navy for demonstrating against Spanish whalers but slipped out of harbour in the dark and escaped. She finally met her end in New Zealand in 1985 when preparing to protest against French nuclear tests at Moruroa in the Pacific. French secret service agents planted a bomb on her hull as she lay against the wharf in Auckland harbour. A Greenpeace photographer, Fernando Pereira, went below to save his cameras just as a second bomb exploded trapping him in his cabin and drowning him. The secret service agents responsible were later arrested and sentenced to ten years' imprisonment but subsequently released by the French government. A second *Rainbow Warrior* has now been commissioned. It may well be asked whether these heroics have served any useful purpose, and indeed they might not have done had not Greenpeace been careful to organise maximum media coverage for their demon-strations.

Any survey of worthwhile conservation organisations would be incomplete without inclusion of the International Fund for Animal Welfare (IFAW). Founded by a Welshman, Brian Davies, the IFAW's foremost concern is the prevention of cruelty. One of its earliest campaigns was against the annual slaughter of the baby harp seals for their white fur that took place in the Gulf of St Lawrence. The fight against the Canadian government lasted for 20 years, during which time Davies was gaoled and hounded out of Canada to take refuge in the United States. Bernhard Grzimek also fought hard for the harp seals, appealing for funds from his German television audience and raising $800 at a crucial point in the campaign. Finally, Davies did win through, persuading the European Parliament to impose a complete ban on the import of seal skins, after which the annual slaughter ceased.

IFAW has gone on to fight many worthwhile campaigns since. One in particular was of great service to wildlife conservation as a whole. At the meeting of the IUCN Survival Service Commission in Costa Rica in March 1979, Dr Marc Dourojeanni, Director General of the Forestry and Fauna Department of the Ministry of Agriculture of Peru, gave a detailed and deeply disturbing briefing on the status of the vicuna in Peru. The vicuna is a small deer-like, high-altitude mammal, distantly related to the camel and carries some of the warmest and finest hair in the world. Unlike other South American cameloids it cannot be domesticated but it can be rounded up for shearing. The hair is then woven into some of the most expensive luxury cloth in the world. Five hundred years ago, there were probably several million vicuna; by 1965 it was reckoned that the world population had been reduced to fewer than 10,000 all of whom lived in the *puna*, the high grazing land of the Andes.

Dr Dourojeanni's report stated that a recent dramatic increase in numbers, coupled with a severe drought, had greatly reduced the grazing and therefore the carrying capacity of their range. It had thus put the lives of thousands of vicuna at risk. Unless drastic action was taken they would starve to death. He ruled out any question of translocation as costs were too high, although it later emerged that no experiments in moving the vicuna had been carried out. Sadly, the only alternative, Dr Dourojeanni maintained, was to 'harvest' the surplus animals and sell the wool and meat products.

The Survival Service Commission had no reason to doubt the facts so they reluctantly agreed to the cull. Before this could be done legally, however, the vicuna case would have to be transferred from Appendix

One (which gives complete protection) to Appendix Two of the Convention on International Trade in Endangered Species (CITES). At the following CITES meeting the well-known South American conservationist, the late Dr Felipe Benavides, an international trustee of the World Wildlife Fund, strongly opposed the proposal which was rejected.

In November that year, IFAW took a hand. Ian MacPhail, now European Co-ordinator of IFAW, together with wildlife veterinary surgeon Dr William Jordan and Tony Morrison, film-maker and authority on Andean wildlife, left for Peru to take a look at the situation on the ground. They found no evidence of drought or over-grazing and no corpses of vicuna who were said to have died of starvation. They did, however, discover chilling and deep-freezing equipment and a refrigerator truck from a modern slaughter-house. There were also plenty of eyewitness accounts of a most inexpert cull having been carried out by inexperienced 'marksman'. Many animals had been shot in the lungs or stomach so as to leave the heart, a great local delicacy, undamaged.

IFAW immediately began a campaign asking its supporters to write to the Peruvian ambassador in their country demanding an end to this cruel and quite needless slaughter. As a result, the killing was stopped by order of the President of Peru, a move supported by IUCN and the World Wildlife Fund which had both originally approved the cull on the strength of the misleading information given by Dr Dourojeanni. No fewer than 8,045 vicuna had by then been killed and their wool and meat sold at great profit, 39 per cent of these animals being pregnant females.

In 1986, experiments were made in capturing vicuna. Few difficulties were found and 30 were successfully moved to Lima Zoo. Four females were pregnant on arrival and produced healthy young. Successful shearing experiments were carried out by New Zealand experts. It now seems highly probable that even if the animals cannot be domesticated, they can be captured, sheared and their wool woven locally into vicuna cloth. This is good practical conservation. It will not only keep the species in existence but also profit the local people who allow their range to be grazed by the vicuna.

Incredibly, Dr Dourojeanni, who had misled the CITES meeting in Costa Rica, became one of the conservation advisers to the World Bank in Washington which has many times been accused by conservationists of providing funds for dams and other huge development projects that, though apparently beneficial in the short term, have ultimately proved destructive of both environment and wildlife.

I have written about the beginnings of the World Wildlife Fund and its immediate aim of saving endangered species. It soon became obvious that no species could be saved unless its environment was also protected. Equally evident was that in a world in which 730 million people are half starving, 1,200 million lack safe drinking water and 2,200 million live on less than £200 per year, there will be a large section of the population that will not view saving wildlife and wild places as a top priority. For the world's poor, economic development is crucial, but development that ruins the environment will only make their plight worse. Yet such change is often avoidable. In 1980 the WWF, IUCN and the United National Environment Programme (UNEP) got together to produce a World Conservation Strategy, the basis of which was to link conservation with development.

This has produced some changes of approach which might conceivably shock some of the well-wishers who drop their coins into the plastic panda collecting boxes. Nevertheless, they are entirely sound and practical. For example, in order to involve and benefit local people, 'buffer zones' have been established around some countries' reserves and parks. Inside these, local people are encouraged to take a sustainable yield of surplus animals. Such a zone has been set up around Korup, Africa's finest rain forest where the native tribes can carry on controlled hunting, fishing, fish farming and agriculture to provide themselves with an income. Every year 360,000 acres of Africa's forests are cleared but, this figure will be reduced if more experiments like that in Korup are implemented.

WWF controversially supports the same attitude to controlled hunting around some national parks in Zimbabwe and on the Kafue flats in Zambia. In recent years, the lechwe antelope there have been reduced from hundreds of thousands to 35,000 due to poaching and over-grazing. Initial government attempts to restrict cattle numbers and stop poaching had little effect. Together with Zambia's Department of National Parks and Wildlife, WWF ran an education programme to show the resident tribes how they could benefit from planned conservation. Now, in consultation with local community leaders, the Department sets annual lechwe hunting quotas – how many lechwe are needed by the tribes and how many may be shot by trophy hunters for $500 a head. The result is that cattle numbers have been reduced, poaching has virtually stopped as it is inconsistent with the residents' interests, and the lechwe population has built up to 50,000.

The WWF's lechwe project has been a success, although not all of its schemes are as productive. The 1990 Phillipson Report, commissioned by the WWF to review its achievements, concluded that while 73 per cent of the Fund's short-term objectives have been achieved over the years, money spent on individual endangered species, notably the elephant and black rhino, had done little to increase their chances of survival. For example, WWF spent £1 million constructing a panda breeding and research centre in China which had turned out to be a total disaster. With the African elephant or the black rhino, there is often little that can be done other than provide funds for anti-poaching measures. The survival of these animals rests, in the end, on the determination of the particular governments. And, though some of the criticism in the Phillipson Report was deserved, what was overlooked by the media was that the Report was, after all, commissioned by the WWF in the first place, presumably to find out where it had gone wrong and how it could become more effective in the future.

Despite some mistakes, the WWF has become the world's most powerful wildlife campaigning force and now has some astute financial advisors from whom has come one of its brightest ideas, the Debt for Nature Swap. A poor, developing country provides local currency bonds for conservation purposes such as the protection of national parks, in exchange for alleviation of some of its foreign debts. In a swap with Ecuador, the WWF bought US $1 million of the country's foreign debt for $350,000 from American banks, or at 35 cents a dollar, a rate that tripled the value of WWF's conservation investment.

Today, WWF's world conservation strategy is based on three main priorities:

1 Preserving the biological diversity of the planet.

Science has so far only identified 1.3 million species. Despite our attempts to wipe them out, there may be as many as 30 million left. No-one knows what benefits those unknown plant and animal species may yet confer on humanity – if only we can save some of them.

2 The saving and rehabilitation of forests and woodlands.

These regulate water supply, bind the soil and prevent erosion, as well as providing a habitat for the greatest number of species.

3 The conservation of wetlands and coast.

Wetlands produce eight times as much vegetation as well-managed farmland. Many commercial fisheries depend on sheltered waters as breeding grounds. The unplanned building of dams can do irreversible damage to river systems, forests and flood plains.

123

However grand the strategy, it is the endangered animals that continue to be the focal point for both private and public support. Even bankers can understand a campaign to save an exciting species whereas detailed ecological arguments may leave their cheque books firmly closed. WWF has launched many such campaigns among which Operation Tiger was a classic example. In 1973, when the tiger project began, there were only 1500 tigers left in India. WWF obtained the backing of the Indian Prime Minister, Indira Gandhi, who was extremely sympathetic to conservation. With the support of the Indian wildlife and parks organisations, 15 tiger reserves were set up with highly successful results. There are now more than 4,000 tigers in India.

Unfortunately tigers, especially the males, require more territory than a reserve often allows them. Inevitably there were cases of cattle being killed; worse, some humans fell victim to man-eaters. The worst cases occurred among the mangrove swamps and coastal forests of the Sunderbans in India and Bangladesh. Though the Sunderbans are a national park, fishermen and honey-hunters still find their living in the forests and around the coast. The locals know that they go into the park at their own risk. Nevertheless, at one point, up to 36 people a year were being killed by tigers.

In terms of conservation, the 500 Sunderbans tigers are crucial. They form the only population large enough to contain a gene pool of sufficient breadth to ensure successful breeding, natural evolution and adaptation.

So ways had to be found to protect the local inhabitants as well as the tigers. The Indian authorities came up with some bizarre ideas, such as models of wood-cutters dressed in worn clothes with a strong human scent and wired up to give an attacking tiger a sharp electric shock. Tigers tore the dummies apart but weren't deterred by the electric shock.

After many failures, cheap plastic face masks were issued to Sunderbans workers to wear on the back of the head. It is said that tigers usually attack when the victim's back is turned. Results were dramatic: 2,500 out of 8,000 workers began wearing the masks. In the first year not one of these was killed by a tiger though 30 without masks became victims.

The story illustrates the fact that no conservation campaign is straightforward and that very few, if any, can avoid a clash between wildlife and human interests.

Success in any conservation project depends on having a large enough body of public opinion behind it. The role of the campaigners, whether individuals like Dian Fossey and Joy Adamson or organisations such as Greenpeace and the World Wide Fund for Nature, is to ensure that the support is there.

12

Goodbye to Them?

There is no doubt that we are saying goodbye to the world's wide variety of life forms at an astonishing rate. Since 1700 at least 69 mammal species have become extinct, 44 of them since 1800. Leading ecologists agree that the present rate of extinction of both flora and fauna is at an average rate of several species a day, at least 1,000 times the pace during the prehistoric past. There are scientists who refer to the present phase of decline as 'an extinction spasm' and liken it to the global wipe-out that put paid to the dinosaurs in the late Cretaceous period, 65 million years ago.

No one can explain the exact cause of that catastrophe. What is certain is that it was not, like the present disaster, man-made. There are other significant differences. It seems that ancestral placental mammals, some birds, non-dinosaurian reptiles and a good deal of the flora survived, giving a basis on which evolution could begin to generate replacement species. That wipe-out undoubtedly spanned several thousand years. The present extinction episode is being crammed into a century or two at the most. In an extremely perceptive article in *Oryx*, the Oxford biologist Norman Myers argues that the obliteration we seem set on achieving could be the greatest blow to biodiversity since life began on earth almost four billion years ago. To put it another way, the destruction that has taken place and is still taking place will all have occurred in .000025 per cent of the time that life has existed on this planet.

Can we do anything about saving what is left and so, by saving the forests, the oceans, the coral reefs, the wetlands, estuaries, rivers and all the other biotopes and consequently the flora and fauna they contain, save ourselves? Myers believes that we can – just – but it will take an awful lot of money and determination.

If we are to do so, a world strategy must be worked out by the best economists, biologists, sociologists and politicians the nations can muster. As to the cost: let us take the efforts of the World Wide Fund for Nature as a base-line. By truly magnificent efforts, WWF has raised since its inception in 1961 about $130 million, or $5 million a year. Compare this with UNO's Food and Agriculture Organisation's estimate for a comprehensive campaign to save the world's dwindling biotopes: $90 million for the first five years to conserve tropical forests; $10 billion per year to improve agriculture among 150 million subsistence farmers – a measure aimed at stemming the flow of landless farmers into wildlife habitats. To halt the spread of desert, $5 billion a year; to supply improved birth control services throughout the Third World $4 billion a year – surely one of the most important moves since world over-population lies at the centre of the entire problem. To improve water supplies and sanitation for 1½ billion of the Third World's poorest people would cost $46 billion annually. The importance of this last is that it would reduce infant mortality and thus lessen one of the incentives for large families (there are, of course other incentives, just as there is great religious and cultural opposition to birth control). These plans are, perhaps, fanciful but the figures, at least, are unlikely to be an over-estimate. The total bill comes to $67 billion a year, just less than twice the current aid to under-developed countries. Can we afford it? Norman Myers comments: 'even if a species conservation programme in itself were to cost several billion dollars a year, this would not be out of line with other major efforts on the part of the global community. Indeed, since species contribute to modern drugs, agricultural crops, industrial materials and energy supplies, it would reinforce the vastly greater investments in human welfare via public health, agriculture and so forth.' Surely, then, the question is: how can we not afford to do it?

I will leave the final words to the late Sir Peter Scott: 'Sadly, I have discovered that there is no hope whatever of saving *all* that I or any other conservationist would like to save, but, if we can work together without internecine strife and keep working hard without losing heart, we shall save a great deal more of our natural world than if we had never tried.'

Notes on the Tsetse Fly

Many national parks in Africa owe their existence solely to the tsetse fly. Its presence makes them totally unsuitable for domestic stock. Superficially, the tsetse resembles a large house-fly. In fact, there is one very obvious difference; most two-winged flies, including the European house-fly, point the rear part of their wings diagonally outward, while the tsetse folds one wing over the other like the blades of a pair of scissors. There are 22 species of tsetse, all belonging to the same genus, *Glossina*, found only in Africa, though 20 million years ago they also survived in America. All tsetse flies feed in the same way, by extracting generous helpings of blood from vertebrates with a dagger-like proboscis that can penetrate even a rhino's hide.

Apart from this painful bite, the flies themselves are harmless, but then so are female anopheles mosquitoes which spread malaria also by biting their blood donors. The tsetse, though, is the carrier of a microscopic parasite called a trypanosome – 'tryp' for short – which, injected into the human bloodstream, can cause sleeping sickness. If detected in the early stages, while still in the blood, the sickness is treatable but, once it reaches the central nervous system it is usually too late to do anything about it. With most other flies, only the females drink blood. Tsetse flies are the exception. Both sexes are blood-suckers.

The symptoms of untreated sleeping sickness, or trypanosmoiasis, are fever, lethargy, delirium and finally coma. Despite vigorous campaigns against the fly, it is estimated that up to 20,000 Africans are afflicted every year; many more cases go undetected. A different sort of tryp affects domestic stock by attacking the red blood cells. The sickness is known as *nagana*. At least three million African cattle die yearly from this disease. Historians say that, one thousand years ago, the Islamic invasion of Africa stopped dead when it reached the fly belt as the Arabs' horses, camels and goats inexplicably started to die. Most wild mammals in Africa carry tryps in their bloodstream, though they have developed immunity except under stress conditions such as famine and prolonged drought. They do, however, form a natural reservoir of tryps as the flies are impartial about whom or what they bite.

The tsetse fly requires a very special habitat. It will not tolerate the cold, so it is absent from high savannah country, preferring the warm, low savannah dotted with thick scrub or woodland. This is exactly the sort of country in which many national parks have been sited. The tsetse has a life-history quite unlike its distant relative the house-fly. The latter lays thousands of eggs which hatch into larvae commonly known as maggots. The pairing of male and female tsetse fly may take up to five hours. The female is then fertilised for the rest of her life. Even if she reaches a place where there are no other tsetse flies she will continue to produce offspring for the remainder of her 200-day existence. She does not, however, lay eggs. Instead she hatches out a single egg inside her body and feeds the larva through special glands. The young then goes through three instars, that is to say it sheds its skin three times while inside the mother's body. The single larva is born as a whitish maggot, two-fifths of an inch long. After its 'birth' the maggot burrows into the ground where it pupates. Thirty-five days later the adult fly emerges, free from parasites. These it picks up when it takes its first meal of blood from an infected body. Once the tryps are in the bloodstream, the host's system starts to produce anti-bodies to combat the onslaught, but single-celled tryp flagellates can change their protective armour, known as antigen coating. The host's forces respond with their new anti-bodies although the tryp is always one jump ahead. This quick-change act has so far defeated medicine in its search for a cure-all vaccine against sleeping sickness and *nagana*.

Physical and chemical means of control have to be used instead. In the past, attempts were made to create no-fly areas by shooting all wild animals inside the tsetse control zone. These exercises proved both wasteful in terms of conservation as well as ineffectual. It is easy to shoot large animals like bushbuck, said to be one of the principle *nagana* hosts, but impossible to account for every bushbaby, mouse and cane rat, all of which can carry tryps.

When I first went to Uganda in 1961, wild animals of many species were still being shot in a futile attempt to control the fly. Huge numbers of animals have been exterminated in other parts of Africa in the same lost cause. Southern Rhodesia, as it then was, had a particularly bad record in this respect. Guns were issued to Africans and bounties paid on animals shot. Between 1932 and 1965, 550,594 wild animals were slaughtered in this way – this doesn't begin to take into account the number that were wounded by inexperienced marksmen and ultimately died. In the late 1960s, tsetse 'control' in Southern Rhodesia accounted for the deaths of 36,552 wild animals including 3,219 baboons, 61 wild dogs, 35 hyenas, 19 leopards, 4 lions, 55 elephants, 8 rhinos, 312 zebras, 950 bush pigs, 4,503 warthogs, 377 buffaloes, 50 wildebeest, 301 waterbuck, 777 reedbuck, 1,327 sable antelope, 306 roan antelope, 291 eland, 4,937 kudu, 5 nyala (a rare antelope), 1,788 bushbuck, 2,219 impala, 12,566 duiker, 1,037 klipspringer, 134 oribi and 1,206 oryx. (The figures are Professor Bernhard Grzimek's, quoted from an official report and can be taken as authentic.)

There were enough animals in that one year's kill to stock a small national park. Those days are happily over but it took a long time for the opinions expressed by Sir David Bruce in his 'Reports of the Sleeping Sickness Commission of the Royal Society' (1915) to lose their force:

> It would seem to be self-evident that these wild animals should not be allowed to live in fly country where they constitute a standing danger to the native inhabitants and their domestic animals. It would be as reasonable to allow mad dogs to live and be protected by law in our English towns and villages. Not only should all game laws restricting destruction in fly country be removed, but active measures should, if feasible, be taken for their early and complete blotting out.

The attack on the tsetse now consists mostly of spraying from the air and on the ground. Harmless insecticides like Endosulfan are used in aerial spraying but too often ground treatment relies on harmful DDT which persists and builds up in the fatty tissues of animals, killing them or making them infertile. It has therefore, thankfully, been banned in most countries being, in any case, costly since the treatment has to be repeated at intervals due to the long period between the female tsetse laying the larva and the fly emerging.

Recently, considerable success in the fight against the tsetse has been obtained by trapping. Chemicals that simulate odours in the breath of domestic stock attractive to the fly are used. The flies are lured by these smells towards a black cloth disc in front of which is an insecticide-impregnated net. A good deal of progress has been made on this method in Zimbabwe and Zambia, although all 38 countries afflicted by the fly have their own research programmes.

Wildlife authorities and conservationists find themselves in two minds about the fly problem. Obviously it is desirable to reduce human infection and, to a lesser extent, cattle disease. Trapping in the vicinity of villages is providing some of the answers but, if the fly is completely wiped out the effect on the environment could be disastrous. Cattle numbers could then escalate at a great pace, and nothing destroys the fragile grazing lands of Africa quicker and more thoroughly than over-use by domestic stock. If this happens and the grasslands degrade, then many sources of food used by Africans will be lost. Not only the large mammals could disappear, but also fish and insects such as termites, grasshoppers and even caterpillars, all of which are eaten at certain times of the year. Because they believe that the continued spread of domestic animals is a major danger to the grazing and soil of much of Africa, some scientists argue that while the tsetse fly population must be carefully controlled, it must not be extinguished.

Notes on
the History and Use
of Light Aircraft

Light aircraft, and latterly helicopters, play a key part not only in operations designed to save threatened animals but in the day-to-day running of national parks. Much scientific work on wildlife would be impossible without them.

The national parks of Africa discovered their uses in the late 1950s and early 1960s but North American conservation organisations had found them indispensable already in the late 1920s and 1930s. There are, after all, huge wilderness areas in the United States and Canadian north that can be surveyed and policed only by air. The men who first flew the US mail in string-and-canvas aircraft like that famous biplane the 'Jenny' (the Curtis JN 4), were exactly the adventurous sort of pilots who took readily to bush flying. America also had a growing aviation industry, some of the products being ideally suited to the rough-and-ready conditions imposed by wildlife work. Since much of this work concerned waterfowl and involved flying over lakes, rivers, swamps and muskeg, many of the aircraft were amphibious like the Grumman Widgeon and, later, the Grumman Goose. Today it is a prerequisite for almost every warden, in these northern waterfowl areas, to be able to fly.

One of the earliest airborne surveyors in the Canadian far-north was Gerry Malaher. He probably spent more hair-raising hours in the air over the far northern wilderness than any of his colleagues. He started flying in open-cockpit amphibians like the Vickers Vedette in the mid-1920s though always as observer and navigator rather than pilot.

One day when on patrol in a Cyrus Mark 2 Moth, an early De Havilland biplane, the magneto packed up. A few miles to the north was a safe landing 'ground' on Happy Lake. Before many seconds had passed it was clear that the Moth was not going to make it. The only alternative was an extremely unattractive muskeg lake. Muskeg lakes are shallow and full of dead vegetation, live weed and submerged roots. When Malaher plumbed the depth with a paddle after landing safely, paddle and arm disappeared into the morass as if plunged unobstructed into water. It took Malaher and his pilot half an hour to make the quarter mile to the shore. The only way they could move forward was by feeling for sunken roots with their toes and placing their feet on them.

In those days, wildlife planes carried two homing pigeons in lieu of a radio. These were released on the shore of Happy Lake.

Next morning a Vedette amphibian landed with the commanding officer of the nearest Canadian Air Force station. The plane was fitted with a new magneto, pulled to the shoreline of the muskeg, stripped of every moveable fitting and drained of all but five gallons of petrol. The aircraft was then tethered by the tail to a small spruce, the engine started and tested. Sergeant 'Egghead' Elliot, the lightest pilot from the station, was put aboard with instructions to open her up to full revs. When he had done this he was to give a signal to cut the tail rope. At full throttle and still tied to the tree, the Moth lifted her pontoons clear of the water and was obviously raring to go. Elliot gave the signal for release and the plane leapt forward but seemed reluctant to leave the surface. At the last moment, 'Egghead' pulled back on the stick and leap-frogged her over the trees into a happy landing on Happy Lake.

★

One of the pioneer waterfowl warden-aviators from Alaska, James G. King, describes the qualities needed by a wildlife pilot:

Not any pilot will do. Most student pilots are taught that speed and altitude are the best friends of small plane pilots and they cringe at the thought of slow speeds and low altitudes. The wildlife pilot knows that his mechanic is his best friend and that if the plane is well cared for, he can live – even when operating low and slow. Having solved these problems, neophyte wildlife pilots still find some hurdles to negotiate. Everything looks strange from above – especially birds, which we normally learn to identify from below or at eye level. Visual targets move past with startling speed even when flying slowly. Learning to make bird observations from the air is like learning speed-reading, trick-shooting or other activities that appear impossible at first but are mastered by persistent practice. Good aerial observers, like musicians, know they must practise regularly.

The best aerial ornithologists are pilots. The pilot can adjust automatically for speed, wind, sun, shadow, elevation and direction, always placing himself where his eyes are most effective – advantages denied passengers no matter how great their experience. Trained wildlife pilots develop a sense of ecology just as a taxicab driver develops a sense of the pulse of a big city denied to his often-mortified passengers. Armed with aeronautical and ornithological proficiency, the wildlife pilot is still not ready to provide a scientifically acceptable product. He must have a system, a survey designed for recording and analysing what he sees.

Much of the work these early pilots did was census-taking of wildfowl populations, often by individual species. They used five basic systems. First, a complete census. This works best with easily seen birds like eagles and swans. Second, the random plot census, used with large and widespread populations. The observer grids the entire area into blocks, selects a block and makes a complete search and record of that sample. Third, the line-transect survey. In Alaska a 16-mile flight path was once chosen, so that the pilot and observer could count birds within an eighth of a mile on each side of the plane. This gave a sample of four square miles for each 16-mile segment flown. The sample was then multiplied to scale it up to the total square miles of habitat in the area. Hunting regulations all over North America have been based on data gained in this way for the past 30 years. Fourth, the random flight method. This really is random but, surprisingly, works pretty well. Anyone flying regularly across bird habitat simply notes on each flight the numbers of selected species seen, and, where possible, their activities. By this method, one experienced observer documented the seasonal behaviour of whistling swans on the Yukon delta over a one-year period with amazing accuracy. He recorded their spring arrival, nest initiation, peak hatching, brood sizes, fledgling and departure in considerable detail. Lastly, the exploratory flight method used by observers flying over unfamiliar territory. With this, it isn't necessary to fly on a straight course as in the line-transect method. The observer simply calculates birds seen per square mile and expands the figure for the total square miles of habitat. This way, in 1966, Alaskan wildlife pilots and observers calculated the number of whistling swans and white-fronted geese on the 23,000 miles of Alaska's arctic slope. The totals, 800 and 50,000 respectively, lacked, in the jargon of the trade, 'statistical credibility'. Later surveys made on a more scientific basis showed the estimates to be surprisingly accurate.

Aerial census taking is, of course, by no means confined to ducks, geese, swans and eagles. Aerial counts are regularly made of plains animals in Africa. Though systems may vary in detail they remain pretty much those described above – as do the requirements of a good wildlife aircraft. Almost invariably they are high-winged for good visibility, have a short landing and take-off capability and a rugged undercarriage to cope with rough terrain. They must be able to fly extremely slowly and to remain in the air while doing so, while having a flight range of five to six hours. In northern latitudes, De Havilland Beavers have met most of these requirements. In other parts of the world Cessna and Piper aircraft are most used. In the early days in Africa many wardens flew Piper Cubs and Supercubs, extremely basic and simple aircraft which Bernhard Grzimek described as looking like a child's toy. So lightly constructed and aerodynamically excellent were they that Murray Watson, one of the biologists working on game counts on the Serengeti in the early 1960s, used to soar a Supercub with the engine switched off out of the Ngorongoro Crater on the up-currents around the rim.

Light aircraft play an important part in spotting and pinning down poachers and are often used as flying aerials to pick up signals from animals wearing radio transmitters.*

* Telemetry, to give it its correct name, means the attachment of very small radio transmitters to selected animals so that their movements can be monitored. It has been used on everything from pheasants and hedgehogs in Britain to elephants and tigers in Africa and India. The batteries of these radios are nowadays recharged by solar power. The radios usually have a maximum range of several miles, so in difficult terrain where it is impossible to pick up their signals by using a directional aerial on foot, a light aircraft or helicopter is the obvious alternative. Recently it has become possible to radio-track larger animals such as polar bears by satellite. Telemetry has become so sophisticated that one can obtain detailed information on behaviour including (with birds) breeding success, from egg-laying to hatching. The diet of the young has even been discovered by using telemetry to locate nests and roosts and then analysing the contents of the droppings on the ground below. Basic data transmitted by telemetry usually includes habitat used, time, date, weather and location. The technique is invaluable in estimating the home-range of an animal.

Notes on Banding Wildfowl

Banding techniques have come a long way since Audubon's day. Wildfowl are possibly the easiest birds to which to attach leg rings, neck bands or sometimes wing tags. Wildfowl have both a physical quality and a behavioural habit that favour the ringer. They are extremely tough and difficult to damage. After breeding they moult all their flight feathers and are therefore grounded for several weeks. During the moult hundreds, sometimes thousands of ducks or geese can be persuaded to walk or swim along a funnelled entrance of netting until they arrive in the trap at the end. Some species are easier to persuade than others. Diving ducks such as the tufted and pochard are notoriously difficult because they can submerge and escape at the crucial moment. Surface or dabbling species, however, can prove tricky; gadwall are especially good at escaping at the last minute. On the prairies of Canada as many as 10,000 ducks have been caught in one drive. These numbers are usually trapped on a 'moulting ground' where several species congregate annually after breeding to shed their main flight feathers or primaries. There is only one drawback to this otherwise convenient arrangement. Ducks on moulting grounds invariably come from several breeding areas. Since they choose different locations for nesting and moulting, there is no way of recording where any individual bird actually nested. Whenever possible an attempt is made to band flightless young on the nesting ground though, obviously, this has to be done with as little disturbance as possible. Netting is also carried out during the birds' passage down the flyway. The ducks and geese are then full-winged and extremely strong. Often, rocket nets are used. The rockets which carry the heavy net up and over the target for a distance of 20 or 30 yards are set up and the net laid out. The area to be netted is baited for several days with food attractive to the species concerned. This may be wheat or maize. Once enough birds have become accustomed to feeding safely on this delicacy, the rockets are fired electrically from a blind or hide. Catches of anything up to 50 geese can be made at one shot. The birds are next checked to see if they are already carrying rings. If not, newly numbered rings are put on their legs, details of age and sex are taken and the birds released. Hunters are required to return either rings or the numbers and details on them to the authority shown on the tag. Later captures by wildlife teams add to the picture. In one year Ducks Unlimited banded 126,800 ducks and 2,600 geese. To this total must be added the many thousands monitored by Canadian, American and Mexican state wardens. The records are kept on computers. Thus an up-to-date and accurate picture can be kept of the rise or fall of the waterfowl population of North America. At the moment of writing (1989) the figures are steady and even increasing despite the mounting pressures on wetlands everywhere.

Select Bibliography

Michael Brander, *The Big Game Hunters*, The Sportsman's Press, 1988.
Mark Cardwardine, *The WWF Environment Handbook*, Optima, 1990.
R. A. Critchley, 'Operation Noah', *Oryx*, 1959.
Brian Davies, *Red Ice*, Methuen, 1989.
The Duke of Edinburgh, *Down to Earth*, Collins, 1989.
Dian Fossey, *Gorillas in the Mist*, Hodder & Stoughton, 1983.
Jane Goodall, *The Chimpanzees of Gombe*, Harvard University Press, 1986.
Bernhard Grzimek, *Rhinos Belong to Everybody*, Collins, 1964.
Bernhard & Michael Grzimek, *Serengeti Shall Not Die*, Collins, 1960.
Janet Kear & A. J. Berger, *The Hawaiian Goose*, T. A. D. Poyser, 1980.
George Lacock, *The Sign of the Flying Goose*, Natural History Press, 1965.
Joseph P. Linduska & Arnold Nelson (editors), *Waterfowl Tomorrow*, U.S. Department of the Interior Fish & Wildlife Service, 1984.
Tom McHugh, *The Time of the Buffalo*, Alfred A. Knopf, 1972.
Harvey Nelson, A. S. Hawkins, R. C. Hanson & H. M. Reeves (editors), *Flyways*, U.S. Department of the Interior Fish & Wildlife Service, 1984.
Goetz Dieter Plage, *Wild Horizons*, Collins, 1980.
Ian Player, *Big Game*, Caltex, 1972.
George B. Schaller, *The Serengeti Lion*, University of Chicago Press, 1972.
Robert Scharf, *Yellowstone and Grand Teton National Parks*, David McKay, 1966.
Bernard Stonehouse, *Saving the Animals*, Weidenfeld & Nicolson, 1981.
Angus Waycott, *National Parks of Western Europe*, Inklon, 1983.
Colin Willock, *The Enormous Zoo: A Profile of the Uganda Parks*, Longmans, 1964.

Index

Index